PRAY THE KINGDOM WAY

A Framework For How to Connect, Co-Create, & Conquer With God For Success In Business

JULIA M. WINSTON

PRAY THE KINGDOM WAY

A Framework For How to Connect, Co-Create, & Conquer With God For Success In Business

JULIA M. WINSTON

Copyright © 2023 by Julia M. Winston

All rights reserved, including the right to reproduce this book or portions thereof in any form whatsoever or by any means. No part of this book may be reproduced, stored in a retrieval system, or transmitted by any means without the written permission of the Author, except as provided by United States of America copyright law.

First Paperback edition June, 2023

Manufactured in the United States of America

Published by Brave Leadership Consulting LLC
www.victoryvision.org

PRINT ISBN: 979-8-9883275-0-9 (paperback)
EBOOK ISBN: 979-8-9883275-1-6 (eBook)

DEDICATION

To my grandmother, the late Rev. Regina Julia Williams, for depositing and demonstrating the power of prayer in my life.

Granny, I love and miss you so much!

ACKNOWLEDGEMENTS

I have to acknowledge some people who were instrumental in getting this released:

Lateef Winston, my love and biggest cheerleader.

Pedro & Suzette Adao and the 100X family, who introduced me to my field of favor.

Dubb Alexander and the School of Kingdom, for giving understanding to my zeal.

The Precision team members: Ingrid, Janine, Annique, Sadie, Melissa, Kelli, Ana, Donald, Crystal, Ruth, Tonya, Bethany, Sherry, Noelle, Christina, and Nannette, who said yes to this crazy vision, who saw this book and called it forth, who are some of the most freakishly accurate prophetic voices in business I know. Thank you. I love the container we built to get businesses breakthrough.

Michelle and Shennice, for being my sister-friends who saw, squealed, and held the light for this.

Michael Dalton, who gave prophetic voice to my destiny.

The "OG" PTKW course community, for allowing me to test on y'all.

To my clients, God is doing some amazing things in business through you. Thank you. We're here for you.

TABLE OF CONTENTS

Preface xi

PART I. 1
Introduction Part I: Important Kingdom Prayer Foundations 3
   1. The Purpose of Prayer in the Kingdom 21
   2. The Kingdom Prayer Framework. 43
   3. Prayers Answered 100% Of The Time. 63

PART II 77
Introduction Part II: For The Kingdom Minded Founder, CEO or
   Leader In Business 79
   4. The Purpose of Business in the Kingdom. 81
   5. Your Business's Identity in Heaven 95
   6. The Purpose of Money in the Kingdom. 111
   7. How To Unapologetically Pray for
      PROFITS Into Your Business 127

Afterword: Business Leaders Rise Up!. .153
Appendix 159
125+ Prayer Prompts, Kingdom Prayer Framework, Sample Prayer
   Journal Page 167
About The Author 173

PREFACE

"Can I teach you to pray?"

~God

Have you ever been asked a life-changing question by God? I have. It was a simple question, yet it shifted my whole perspective on prayer. At the time of this question, I was already deeply connected to prayer.

It started in my childhood with my grandmother. She and her female pastor and ministry friends had the "Prayer Line" every morning. They used three-way calling to get as many praying women as they could on the phone to intercede. I distinctly remember she'd start her sing-song prayer off with her famous, "Oh God, my Master, we come before you today…" and then she'd bring EVERYTHING before Him. I couldn't hear every word from my bedroom upstairs, but I could always hear her say, "Touch'em Lawd," quite loudly.

I was just a child, trying to get a few more minutes of sleep before getting ready for school, when all that was happening. Growing up, I don't ever remember seeing my grandmother read her Bible, although she did, but I always remember hearing her pray. This was the foundation of my lifelong connection with prayer. In college, a disgruntled dorm neighbor reported me to the RA because I was praying too loudly. Those were fun times. Naturally, I would dedicate my first book about prayer to her, because thanks to her, my personal connection with prayer has deep roots. I have been in every type of Christian prayer meeting there is. I have read the books from the great generals of prayer.

The timing of God's question is significant to this book. I knew this was no ordinary question. It was coming at a moment of transition in my life. I was a full-time entrepreneur dedicated to helping Christian CEOs, Executives, and Founders leverage their faith as a source of not just connection to God, but as an untapped resource of innovation and ingenuity in business.

I was introduced to what it means to be in the Kingdom of God through Myles Munroe's *Rediscovering the Kingdom*. From there, I joined Pedro Adao's online community of Kingdom Entrepreneurs called 100X. Pedro connected the Kingdom, business, and the prophetic in a way I had never seen before. Through him, I was introduced to Dubb Alexander and would deepen my understanding of the Kingdom in Dubb's School Of Kingdom. The revelation of the Kingdom changed EVERYTHING.

Inside of 100X, my gratitude for "finding my peeps" was so deep; I was compelled to give back to the community in some way. There were many technical things I couldn't do, but I knew how to do one thing well. I could pray.

As Pedro began traveling to more places and promoting online, I felt compelled to pray for him.

I entered the 100X private online community and asked if others would join me on Zoom™ to pray for Pedro and the events he had coming. Pretty soon, the community began asking me when the next prayer time was going to be. The requests were for a frequency that I could not sustain alone, so I organized and recruited. I asked a select group of people if they would commit to hosting a prayer call once a week for eight weeks. That was how the 100X prayer movement started.

Three years later, we've held over 1,000 prayer calls in our community, with hundreds of Kingdom entrepreneurs in attendance, and about 150 Kingdom entrepreneurs worldwide trained in how to pray the Kingdom way for business. At the same time, I came across Shae Bynes and the Kingdom-Driven Entrepreneur community which had been in existence several years prior. I realized Kingdom entrepreneurship was a move of God on the earth and different people had different pieces they were called to contribute to it. My piece was an understanding of prayer that would help Kingdom entrepreneurs thrive in business.

In my own business, I started an online Prayer Challenge for business owners. Through 100X, my challenge, my course "Pray The Kingdom Way," and my private consulting of Kingdom business leaders, I've trained close to 1,000 Kingdom business owners in more than 50 different business sectors on what I am going to share with you in this book with documentable success.

When God asked, "Can I teach you to pray?" of course my response was a resounding YES!

When I felt prompted to write this book, I asked myself, do we really need another book on prayer?

The answer is Yes!

I wrote this book with a specific audience in mind: business people, business leaders, and CEOs. Why? For one, it was a directive from God. But also, there's a current move of God happening in the business world, and I believe YOU have a role to play in it.

This book is for those who want to pray with more precision, hear from God more clearly, and see better outcomes in their business dealings. And the best part? You can do it all without feeling guilty or wondering if you are exploiting the Gospel. Whether you're a Founder CEO looking to align your heart with God's, or a Kingdom entrepreneur seeking an ROI on Earth as it is in Heaven, this book is for you.

This book has two parts. In the first part of this book, I give you the Kingdom Prayer Framework. Think of it as a quick start guide. I want you to get the meat right at the beginning so even if you don't finish the book, you already have the framework to begin shifting your prayers NOW.

In the second part of the book is the deeper dive into the revelation God gave me about business and money. It includes business-specific examples on how all of this applies to business success. God is moving in business and He's equipping his leaders in business with His mind, His voice, and His intention, and it all unlocks for you when you learn to Pray The Kingdom Way.

PART I

INTRODUCTION

IMPORTANT KINGDOM PRAYER FOUNDATIONS

What you believe about God determines how you interact with Him, what you accept from Him, and what you expect from Him.

I'm a big movie fan and God speaks to me through movie lines all the time. I will use several movie references throughout this book. In the 1987 movie, *Princess Bride*, Vizzini frequently yells, "Inconceivable!" and finally Inigo Montoya says, "You keep using that word. I do not think it means what you think it means." I want to begin by giving some underlying principles and definitions, so you know what I mean when I use certain words. This introduction is not meant to be an exhaustive deep dive into any of these concepts. Many others have written extensively on these concepts, and I encourage you to learn from them. My intention for this book is to unpack these concepts as foundations for Kingdom Prayer.

Foundation #1: God Is Love and God Is Good

God the Father is, always has been, and always will be love.

We see it in several verses throughout scripture.

> *"For God so loved the world that He gave his one and only Son, that whoever believes in Him shall not perish but have eternal life."* (John 3:16 NIV)

> *"So we know and rely on the love God has for us. God is love. Whoever lives in love lives in God and God in them."* (1 John 4:16 NIV)

> *"But you, Lord, are a compassionate and gracious God, slow to anger, abounding in love and faithfulness."* (Psalm 86:15 NIV)

> *"No, in all things we are more than conquerors through Him who loved us."* (Romans 8:37 NIV)

For you to really understand anything in the Kingdom, you must be congruent with this idea that God is love and that He loves you.

God the Father is, always has been, and always will be good!

> *"The Lord, the Lord God, merciful and gracious, longsuffering, and abounding in goodness and truth."* (Exodus 34:6 NKJV)

> *"Oh, give thanks to the Lord for He is good! For His love endures forever."* (1 Chronicles 16:34 NIV)

> *"Good and upright is the Lord."* (Psalm 25:8 NIV)

> *"No one is good but One, that is, God."* (Mark 10:18 NKJV)

> *"Every good gift and every perfect gift is from above, and comes down from the Father of lights, with whom there is no variation or shadow of turning."* (James 1:17 NKJV)

> *"If you then, being evil, know how to give good gifts to your children, how much more will your Father who is in Heaven give good things to those who ask Him!"* (Matthew 7:11 NKJV)

> *"Oh, taste and see that the Lord is good; blessed is the man who trusts in Him!"* (Psalm 34:8 NKJV)

> *"Or do you despise the riches of His goodness, forbearance, and longsuffering, not knowing that the goodness of God leads you to repentance?"* (Romans 2:4 NKJV)

God was love and God was good before fear, hate, and evil ever existed. He is not loving and good *because* fear, hate, or evil exist. He is not loving and good *in response* to fear, hate, or evil. He was and is and is to come. Since His nature predates all things, His original intention for all things created was birthed from the fullness of who He is—loving and good.

If you do not unequivocally believe that God is love AND that He loves you, you will not be able to see His many acts of love towards you. And if you do not believe that God is good, you will not trust Him with the good things that you desire most. What you believe about God determines how you interact with Him, what you will accept from Him, and what you will expect from Him. What you believe about Him determines how you see scripture, the world, yourself, and business. As Kingdom ambassadors, we must have the viewpoint of our homeland when interacting with everything He created.

There are levels to this thing. There are areas, instances, and incidents in your life where believing in God's love and goodness is not a problem. Likewise, there are areas, instances, and incidents where believing His love and goodness is more challenging.

My husband and I have been married for over 20 years. I tell people that the decision to marry him was one of the easiest decisions of my life. I have fretted MORE over my hair and my clothes than choosing to spend the rest of my life with him. God told me in prayer that we'd get married, and I wisely kept it to myself until after the wedding. I not only trusted

God in that area; I trusted Him completely. I knew there was a man out there for me who would meet all my heart's desires. I had full confidence and trust in His love and goodness to me and that He would send me the spouse I desired. I didn't know He'd send him from suburban Oklahoma, but hey.

However, when it came to my career or what I would do professionally, I struggled to trust God. It took me a while to grow into my career and to understand where I was going and what God wanted me to do. The more I got rejected, the easier it was to doubt God's goodness and love. Conversely, I had a dear friend who had deep trust in God's love and goodness for her when it came to her career. She had trusted that God would do remarkable things when it came to her career, but when it came to her relationships with men, trusting God was a harder issue for her. I knew how to trust God for marriage, but not my career. She knew how to trust God for her career, but not for marriage. Can you think of areas in your life where you can undoubtedly see God's love and goodness? I'm sure you can. Likewise, you'd also agree that there are areas where it is harder for you to see His love and goodness, yes?

The good news is that my friend and I are both prospering now. I am married; she is married. She has a great career; I have a great career. There are areas in our lives where we can always grow in our faith in His goodness and love. He will always bring light to the areas where He wants us to trust Him further.

Part of trust is knowing the character of the person with whom you are extending this trust. If you do not think that God's character is good, that God's character is loving, then that will determine how you interact with Him. You will push away things He wants to draw you closer to.

When you do not believe God is love, you will always be suspicious of His motives and intentions toward you. If you do not believe He is loving, then you will not *see* His loving acts towards you because you will look at those loving acts through the lens of suspicion. When you look at loving acts through the lens of suspicion, you will not accept them. If you don't accept them, you won't see them and thus won't reap the benefit of them.

When you do not believe that He is, has been, and always will be good, you may think He is apathetic, indifferent, bad, mean, vindictive, petty, or bored. You will believe that He has no passion, that He is passive. That is not the truth. All that negative thinking robs you of your ability to step fully into faith. It robs you of your ability to step into confidence and joy.

It is really hard to pray to a God you don't believe is good, loving, or trustworthy. It is really hard to get close to a God whose character you don't trust. It makes one cynical and suspicious, and that's a draining place.

The serpent played a trick on Adam and Eve in the garden (Genesis 3:1 NKJV). He tested Jesus on the mountain, and today he pesters you and me with the exact same goal: to get you to *agree* that what you know about God is not true (Matthew 4:8 NKJV). If the enemy can make you suspicious, then that is all he needs to do. Understand that God is omniscient and omnipresent. That means He knows all things, and He is present at all places, all the time, at the same time. Satan is not; the system of darkness is not all-knowing, and it is not all-present. Satan is a created being, a fallen angel. None of the created angels that fell with Satan are superior to God. They are created beings; therefore, they cannot be in all places at all times. They are also not aware of all things. They have one strategy. What is that strategy? The strategy is the whisper of suspicion. Satan cannot tell you what to think because you, as a human being, have greater authority on the earth than he does. I will talk more about that in the later chapters. Just know, the way God set things up on Earth, humans have been given authority to rule, and things happen or don't happen in spiritual partnership with humans. The enemy knows this, so since he can't *make* you think a certain way, he will suggest things for you to think. The moment you agree with his suggestion, he is then given permission to exert his power. When he can get you to put on the lens of suspicion, he can move on and bother someone else because he no longer has that particular work to do; you are doing it for him. He can go on about his business. The goal is the same: to get you to agree that what you know about God is not true.

It is important to stand on truth—the truth that God is love, that God is good. The reason that we struggle with that is because we have come into agreement with the enemy and have had validating experiences that need to be reframed. Romans 12:2 talks about transforming the mind, so we must renew our minds in the areas where we believe and have had experiences where we believed God was not loving or that He was not good. If you had a prayer experience that didn't turn out the way you wanted and it left you hurting and doubting God's goodness and love, then Chapter 3 is for you. Let me encourage you. He is good and he is loving. You may have to walk through informing and transforming your mind about God in those areas, but I promise it is worth it.

Foundation #2: Jesus Is Lord Of ALL Creation

One of my favorite lines from the 2005 *Chronicles of Narnia* movie was delivered by Aslan to the White Witch. After privately negotiating a trade, the White Witch started to remind Aslan of the law if he reneged on his word. He interrupted her with his booming growl and said, "Do not cite the deep magic to me, Witch! I was there when it was written!" Talk about a mic drop moment. I still get chills because it reminded me of Jesus. Jesus is at the center of all creation. He is the *logos-WORD*. The scripture says it this way:

> *"All things were made through Him, and without Him nothing was made that was made."* (John 1:3 NKJV)

> *Christ is the visible image of the invisible God. He existed before anything was created and is supreme over all creation, for through Him God created everything in the heavenly realms and on earth. He made the things we can see and the things we can't see—such as thrones, Kingdoms, rulers, and authorities in the unseen world. Everything was created through Him and for Him.* (Colossians 1:15-16 NLT)

Everything that was created by God was created through and for Jesus. If something is a created thing, it was created pure and purposed in Jesus before it ever came to being. This is an important foundation because as we go deeper in this book, I will share how prayer, business, and money are created things. Since they are created things, then their true origin existed in Christ before we ever discovered it on Earth. If their origin existed in Christ, then they are good.

Much of what I learned about prayer growing up was caught more than taught. Prayer is a participation sport after all. You will never get "better" at it just by observing. My observation began with my grandmother. It continued with various prayer meetings, books, sermons, and teachings on prayer. But I had a flawed foundation when it came to prayer. I basically boiled it down to this: prayer is a spiritual discipline—in other words, something you don't like doing—that takes great effort, and if you do it "right," you *might* get the outcome you want.

Is it any wonder that prayer meetings are the least attended meetings at most churches? Why pray if God is going to do what He wants anyway? That was a question I had for a long time. I believed that the "watchmen" needed to be on the wall, diligently scouting for evil to defend against it, because if we didn't "watch and pray," then the enemy had permission to run freely and kill, steal, and destroy any and everything. As time went on, I prayed more out of a duty than connection with God. I saw prayer as insurance, something you paid into in the hope that nothing bad would happen. And if something bad did happen, and you prayed "right," you might be able to cash in on the benefits. Don't judge me. I'm just telling you my story.

When I was in my late teens, I heard a television pastor say something that disturbed me for decades. He was talking to his congregation about attending the prayer sessions before a big revival or conference that was coming up at his church. As he implored the people to attend the meetings, he began talking about the importance of prayer. He began talking about how we need each other's prayers. He then told a story about an injury or accident his son sustained. Then he said the words that haunted my soul for years. He said, "Who knows? If you would have prayed, perhaps he wouldn't have gone through that." I was shocked. He didn't say it outright. But I thought to myself, *Did this man just blame his church for his son's tragedy?* That emotional pull probably guilted many people into attending the prayer meetings for that event. I never watched that preacher again. It didn't sit well with me. In my own journey, I recognized that the threat of tragedy was often the tactic used to get more people to pray. When I saw that manipulation firsthand, it hindered my prayer life. I still prayed, but the joy was gone, and worse yet, it cast suspicion on God. How could a good God do that? Allow that?

I share this story for any of you who feel guilty about learning to pray better or pray more. I have good news for you. I am not going to lay a guilt trip on you, and I am definitely not going to manipulate you into praying with fear tactics or emotional manipulation. In fact, the foundation section is important because when you pray the Kingdom way, praying becomes more enjoyable for you. Praying without ceasing won't feel like you're being set up to continually miss the mark. You will see it as perpetual connection, co-creation, and conquering with God. Prayer is a created thing, as such, it was created in and through Jesus. Therefore, God, Jesus, and Holy Spirit know exactly what prayer is and how it functions. This is good news for you and how you see prayer.

Foundation #3: Reason And Purpose

In order to get the best from any created thing, one must know the reason and purpose for which it was created. I will talk a lot about reason and purpose in this book, and I define it very specifically.

> ***Reason reflects the heart of the creator.***
> ***Purpose reflects the function of the creation.***

When I use the word reason, I am referring to identifying what was on the creator's heart when he or she created. A reason gives an explanation or justification from the creator. That explanation or justification can tell you a lot about the creator's "original intent." If God created prayer, we have to ask ourselves what His intent was so we can determine if we're aligned with its purpose.

When I use the word purpose, I am referring to identifying the function for which a thing was created. The creator of the microphone had a reason for creating it. The purpose of a thing reflects the function of it. The purpose of a microphone is to amplify sound. If it is not amplifying sound, it is not operating in its purpose. If you took a handheld microphone, for instance, and used it to stir your morning coffee, you absolutely could do that. However, you are not using it according to its purpose, and at best, it's weird; at worst, if it's plugged in, it's dangerous.

In Disney's *The Little Mermaid,* Ariel asks Scuttle about an item she found. Scuttle, a seagull—not the creator of the item—tells her it is called a "dinglehopper" and that says its purpose is for human hairdos. When Ariel, now on land, gets to the dining table and sees the "dinglehopper" on the table next to the spoon, she begins to use it according to the wrong function told to her. A dinglehopper is indeed a fork, and forks are used for eating.

In this example, we see the misappropriation of reason and purpose clearly. The reason the fork was invented reflected something in the creator's heart (to solve a problem, to eat without getting their hands dirty, etc), and the purpose of the fork gave the fork its proper function.

When it comes to prayer, we've had a lot of "Scuttles" telling us about what prayer is and isn't. Few have consulted its Creator to understand how prayer shows God's love and goodness and how prayer has a unique function on Earth. More on that in the upcoming chapters though.

Foundation #4: What Is The Kingdom?

"But seek first the Kingdom of God…" (Matt 6:33 ESV)

Now that we understand that God is love, God is good, God gave Jesus rulership over all creation, and that reason and purpose are two different but related things, let's move on to our final foundation point.

You have to understand what the Kingdom of God is. The Kingdom of God has a good and loving God who has a reason and purpose for everything. Matthew 6:33 tells us to seek first the Kingdom …but what is it? In Greek, the word for Kingdom in that scripture is *basileia*. This word means royal power, kingship, dominion, and rule. It implies the right or authority to rule something.

Since Kingdom is a word that can mean and be used in different ways, I want to be clear about how I will use the word in this book. When Kingdom is used in this book, it means God's original intent and rulership. In his seminal book *Rediscovering the Kingdom,* Myles Munroe notes that the only thing Jesus preached was the Kingdom of God. He goes on to define the Kingdom as "the sovereign rule of a king over territory (domain), impacting it with his will, purpose, and intent."[1] One of my Kingdom friends and mentors, School of Kingdom Founder Dubb Alexander, defines the Kingdom of God as *"The extension of God's heart and mind on Earth through us."*[2]

All these definitions point to a single point: God is the ruler with an optimal way to rule in a place. That "way to rule" is called a governing system. It is the way He does things, and the place that He chooses to exert that system, to display that system, is Heaven. Then He decided that what is in Heaven, He wanted on Earth. Let's look at Genesis.

> *Then God said, "Let Us make man in Our image, according to Our likeness; let them have dominion over the fish of the sea, over the birds of the air, and over the cattle, over all the earth and over every creeping thing that creeps on the earth."* (Genesis 1:26 NKJV)

God says that mankind has dominion over the earth. The Kingdom of God is a governing system that He established. Earth is the territory where mankind is to rule. Because we are made in God's image, we as mankind are an extension of God's rulership and authority here on Earth. This means that the atmosphere of Heaven, the provision of Heaven, and the way things are done in Heaven are what God wants us to replicate here on Earth.

---

[1] (Munroe, 2004)
[2] (Alexander, 2021)

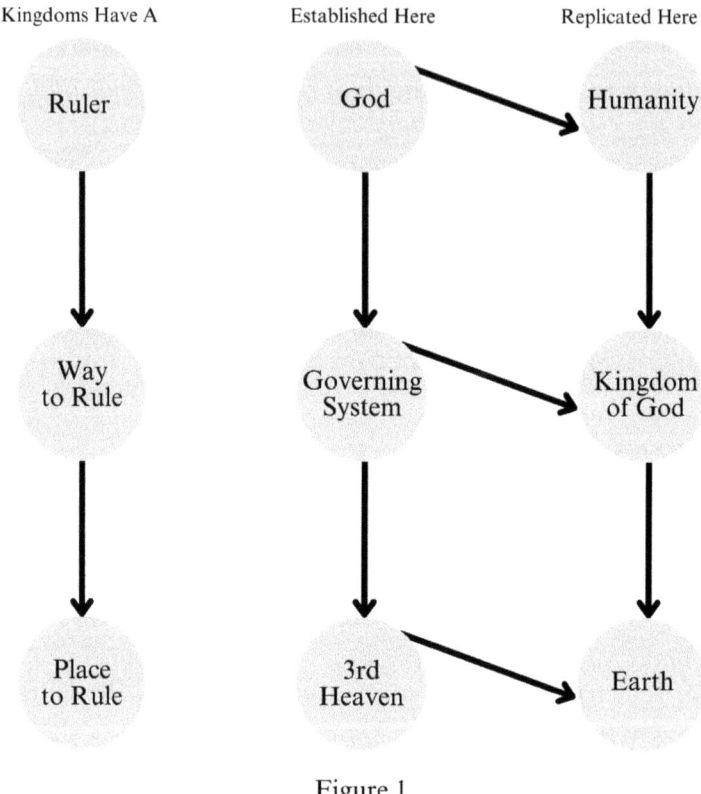

Figure 1

That's why the scripture says that we are ambassadors. Ambassadors are official representatives of one government inside another. Ambassadors represent the will and interests of their homeland while away from home.

God's plan is to establish a family, to establish a government, and to expand both.

God's plan was, and still is, to establish a family, establish a government, and expand both. Because God never wanted to establish a religion, ambassador Jesus never wanted to establish a religion. Because God wanted a relationship with you, ambassador Jesus preached about knowing God as Father. He wants a deep relationship with each and every one of us.

> *"But as many as received Him, to them He gave the right to become children of God."* (John 1:12 NKJV)

God has always wanted a family. He exists for relationship with you. That is why He created man. There is a reason and purpose for your creation. The reason was for love; the purpose was for dominion. His greatest desire was to have relationship with you, a familial relationship with you. When we go back to Genesis it states, *"Let Us make man in Our image, according to Our likeness"* (Genesis 1:26). What was happening?

If we look behind the curtain, we see that God created Earth before He created man. The scripture above gives a peek into the relational aspect that is the Trinity. God has always existed in relationship. Relationship is incredibly important to God; it is paramount to Him. He always existed in this model of family. The Trinity exists in family—the Father, the Son, and Holy Spirit.

> *"So then you are no longer strangers and aliens, but you are fellow citizens of the saints and members of the household of God."* (Ephesians 2:19 ESV)

Who lives in your household? Your family does. We are not strangers. We are not aliens. We are family. We are a royal priesthood. He calls us sons and daughters. He wanted to establish a family and establish a government. Dubb Alexander also says that the *Kingdom of God is familial in nature, but governmental in structure.*[3]

> *"For unto us a Child is born, Unto us a Son is given; And the government will be upon His shoulder."* (Isaiah 9:6 NKJV)

---

[3] (Alexander, From the Cult to the Kingdom, 2021)

What is the purpose of a government? The purpose of government is to create the system through which people under the government will operate. It is the governing system. The play *Hamilton* is about one of the founders of the government of the United States of America, Alexander Hamilton. As the first Secretary of the U.S. Treasury, Hamilton is credited with building a financial foundation for the new nation.

> *"Having been built on the foundation of apostles and prophets, Jesus Christ Himself being the chief cornerstone, in whom the whole building, being fitted together, grows into a holy temple in the Lord."* (Ephesians 2:20-21 NKJV)

The foundation was laid, and Jesus was supposed to be the cornerstone of this government; He is. You must understand something: the word *apostles* and the word *minister* are governmental terms. If you go to any country or nation, you will find the Minister of Defense, the Minister of the Treasury, and so on. Apostleship is about establishing and building. We have relegated these terms to be church terms, but they are governmental terms. The Ecclesia is a governmental body.

> *"Of the increase of His government and peace there will be no end."* (Isaiah 9:7 NKJV)

When God gave the mandate to Adam and Eve in the garden, the whole point was to establish this government.

He said, *"Be fruitful, multiply, subdue the earth, have dominion"* (Genesis 1:22 NKJV). Why? What does that mean? It means God desires expansion.

> *"And then He told them, 'Go into the world and preach the Good News to everyone.'"* (Mark 16:15 NLT)

God's heart is for advancement and expansion. Jesus came to redeem the fall. Redeem means to bring back to the original intent. What was the original intent? The original intent of man was to live in a family and expand the government.

In his book *Rediscovering the Kingdom*, Myles Munroe writes,

> *"God's Kingdom is different from earthly Kingdoms in that it has no subjects. There are no peasants in the Kingdom of God, only sons and daughters. In the Kingdom we are not subjects, but members of a royal family. You are a royal priesthood, a chosen generation."*[4]

If we look at current monarchies, we might say, "Wait a minute. I don't know if I like that because a king has subjects, and I don't want to be a subject." Well, it is not so in the Kingdom of God. There are no minorities in the Kingdom because we are all sons or daughters. In America, we call women and people of color "minorities." Those of you who have children, please point to one of your children and tell me which one of them is a minority in your family. Which one of your children is a second-class citizen in your family? If you are a good parent, your answer will intrinsically be that none of them are minorities! All my children have the exact same equal rights in my house. So it is with sons and daughters in the Kingdom of God. The Kingdom of God does not have subjects; it has family. It is familial in nature but governmental in structure. It is a government.

God wanted to establish a family, but Satan wanted to establish slaves. Because he is an imitator, he does not create life; he destroys it. Jesus said, *"The thief does not come except to steal, and to kill, and to destroy. I have come that you may have life"* (John 10:10 NKJV). In John 8:34,

---

[4] (Munroe, Resdiscovering the Kingdom, 2004)

Jesus said, *"Most assuredly I say to you, whoever commits sin is a slave of sin"* (NKJV). Satan wants us in this sin state because it keeps us slaves. A slave to what? A slave to not knowing our sonship. A slave to feeling as if we are separated from God and the knowledge of our true identity and authority.

> *"We know that our old self was crucified with Him in order that the body of sin might be brought to nothing, so that we no longer be enslaved to sin."* (Romans 6:6 ESV)
>
> *"For freedom Christ has set us free; stand firm therefore, and do not submit again to a yoke of slavery."* (Galatians 5:1 ESV)

Why is Paul saying these words? Because in the family you are free; there are no orphans. Satan wants to establish slaves, and he wants to establish orphans. Orphans have a father, but they either do not know who that father is, or that father is no longer present.

Satan also wants to establish a government.

> *"Again, the devil took him to a very high mountain, and showed him all the Kingdoms of the world and their glory. And he said to him, 'All this I will give you, if you will fall down and worship me.'"* (Matthew 4:8-9 ESV)
>
> *"For wide is the gate and broad is the road that leads to destruction, and there are many who go in by it."* (Matthew 7:13 NKJV)

The enemy wants to expand destruction. He wants to expand anything that can steal, kill, or destroy. A lot of the issues that we are seeing in our world today are spiritual in that they are physical representations of spiritual things.

I believe that the issue of prayerlessness in the body of Christ has more to do with misinterpretation of God, His way of doing things, and purpose with than it does laziness, lack of discipline, or rebellion. If you don't agree that God is loving and good, that He made Jesus supreme over all creation, that He has the ultimate right to give something purpose, then you will have a hard time accepting the framework of prayer offered in this book.

However, if you accept the aforementioned foundation, then you are about to experience a transformation in your thinking about God, you, prayer, business, and money that will make you an unstoppable force in this world. If that sounds good, let's dive in.

CHAPTER 1

THE PURPOSE OF PRAYER IN THE KINGDOM

Who gets to define what prayer is? The one who created it. If you think mankind created prayer to access God, then you will look to mankind to learn the tenets, practices, habits, and customs of prayer. This is what most of our prayer customs have done, and it has made prayer a heavy, burdensome, guilt-ridden thing in the life of mankind.

1 Thessalonians 5:17 says to "...pray without ceasing." In my formative years of prayer, I never understood how that was possible. How could someone actually pray without ceasing? People had to go to work. I had to go to school, I thought. They had to rest, play, and have fun. It was preached very hard that we ought always to pray, and since I never could reconcile how to pray without ceasing and live a normal life, I never felt like my prayer life was good enough. I always felt like I missed the mark on prayer because I wasn't "praying without ceasing."

In fact, let's do an experiment right now. Which statement would you say best describes your attitude about your prayer life?

1. My prayer life is weak.
2. My prayer life is OK.
3. My prayer life is strong, but it could be improved
4. My prayer life is top notch. No improvement needed.

Most people never choose option 4. We believe that our prayer life could always be improved. If you believe your prayer life could use improvement, whether by a lot or a little, then it means you are living in lack and deficiency in your prayer life. That's the residue of traditional prayer from the perspective of prayer created by man.

If mankind created prayer, then the reason for prayer is to connect man to God. If mankind created prayer, then the purpose for prayer is to convince God to do or approve what man asks or wants. If man created prayer, then man gets to tell you how to do it. And over the years, I had a lot of "man" telling me what to do.

Did you get on your knees? Fold your hands? Close your eyes? Enter the gates with thanksgiving first? Confess your sins? Wash at the "lavar"? Pray using the scriptures? Say, "In the name of Jesus"? Say, "In the name of the Father, Son, and the Holy Spirit"? Say, "In the name of Yeshua"? Say the Lord's Prayer? Say the prayer of Jabez? Fast to give extra power to your prayers? Pray long enough? In a closet so no one saw you?

Let's follow this thought for a minute. If man created prayer, and prayer's purpose is to convince God to do what you ask, then if you don't see God do what you asked, man can do one of two things:

> (1) convince you that you are doing it wrong and make you focus on making yourself more righteous in order to see the outcomes. This often comes in the form of accusing you of some secret sin in your life or that your belief wasn't high enough or that you didn't do it long enough, hard enough, or fervent enough.
>
> (2) invent more rules for you to follow in order to get the outcome you want. This often comes in the form of new prayer models to follow. It comes with more nuances, more steps, and more time.

If man created prayer, then man can say you didn't do it *right* and thus tell you what needs to be done to fix it. Fixing it then becomes the onus of man, not God. Onus is used to refer to someone's duty or responsibility, the obligation to prove. It indicates with whom the burden of proof lies. In the legal system of the United States, our justice is built on a presumption of innocence. This means it is the onus of the prosecution to prove beyond doubt that a defendant is guilty. Because of this onus, if the defendant is convicted, it means the prosecution met its burden of proof. If the defendant is acquitted, it doesn't necessarily mean the defendant didn't do it, it means the prosecution couldn't prove it in accordance with the law and regulations of the court.

If man created prayer, then it is man's onus to define and perfect it. We do this by focusing on cultural norms, habits, stylings, practices, and rituals to ultimately prove we are qualified to pray, and by extension, worthy to have our prayers answered.

Man-made prayer positions you as a slave who has no idea what your Master is doing. Man-made prayer teaches that it is not for us to know. *"God, if it is your will, and I don't know if it is or not, please make it so."* Man-made prayer has us tossing things up against a wall to see what will stick.

Man-made prayer means you must prove your worthiness. *"If I get on my knees, and I fold my hands, get up at 3:00 a.m. or stay up late, say the Prayer of Jabez, enter the courts of Heaven, or say the prayers of forgiveness, then maybe God will hear me."*

Ok, time out! Just reading the list above is exhausting, and it feels heavy, right? No wonder people don't want to pray. No wonder people never know if they are doing it "right."

Could it be that people do not pray because religion has made it so complicated and, because of that complexity, it is hard to know if prayer works? Or, if they believe it works, then they always question if they did enough to earn an answer. They say, *"Well, I don't know if I proved myself worthy enough or not. I haven't really talked to God today, so now that I need to ask Him for something, He's probably not going to answer because I haven't talked to Him, so it is my fault."* All that keeps us under of guilt and condemnation. It becomes more about rules than relationship.

Man-made prayer keeps us guessing so much that answers to prayers become a surprise, not an expectation. When our prayers are answered, we feel like we hit the lottery and have no idea why. I came across a Lifeway survey that said that only 25% of people who pray say that their prayers are *always* answered. Fourteen percent of people say they do not know if their prayers are answered, and everyone else fell into the categories of either sometimes their prayers are answered, or most of the time their prayers are answered.[5] What is going on? Why is it a crap shoot?

However, 1 John 5: 3 tells us that *"...the commands of Jesus are not burdensome."* The scripture says in Romans 8:1 that there is no condemnation to those in Christ walking in the spirit. Yet, if you didn't select option 4, then there is a high chance you are feeling condemned about prayer. When I read 1 John 5:3, in relation to prayer, I said, *"Jesus, prayer has always felt burdensome to me. So, either You're wrong or I am."* He said, *"prayer is not burdensome."* In fact, in Matthew 23:4 (NKJV), Jesus accused the Pharisees of burdening the people. It says, *"For they bind heavy burdens, hard to bear, and lay them on men's shoulders…"* Jesus judged the Pharisees for complicating things. They added so many laws, rules, and regulations that it was hard for anyone to fulfill. But in Matthew 11:28-30 (NKJV), Jesus tells the burdened to come to Him for His yoke is easy and His burden is light.

So, if prayer was created by man, why would Jesus condemn the rules man set up for the thing it created?

---

[5] (Smietana, 2014)

PRAYER WAS GOD'S IDEA

Going back to our foundation, everything that was made was made in Him and for Him. Therefore, I submit to you that prayer was not created by man. Prayer is a God idea created in Jesus for use on Earth. This is why Jesus could tell us how and how not to do it. If Jesus wants to unburden us, and prayer feels burdensome, then it stands to reason that there are some things you believe about prayer that are not in line with Jesus's commands because His commands are not burdensome.

Praying the Kingdom way means praying from a different posture. The Kingdom way of praying positions you as a son/daughter in right relationship with your Father because God comes to establish a family, a government, and to expand both. It already demonstrates your worthiness. Jesus made you worthy. I do not have to prove it. The way I pray, the way I connect with the Lord, and the way I show up demonstrates my worthiness. It brings clarity to areas of confusion, and it seats you and me at the table.

Instead of being a slave in the slave quarters with 'massah' up at the big house making all the decisions, you are at the table in collaboration, not just with your fellow Kingdom citizens, but also with the Trinity. You are at the table of collaboration with Jesus, the Holy Spirit, and Father God about the intent, purpose, and desire of your heart and theirs. You are *seated* at the table in collaboration and co-creation. Praying the Kingdom way is about the highest and purest exhibition of relationship over rules or the formula.

Answers can then be expected because you created the prayer with the One who created prayer and wants to bring a result here on Earth. In the Kingdom, you do not pray *for* a Third Heaven perspective; you pray *from* a Third Heaven perspective.

Traditional prayer has you praying from an earthbound perspective, trying to reach Heaven, and hoping that you do. Kingdom prayer has you seated in Heaven already. Which position would you rather have? Would you rather be a beggar hoping God will do something for you, or would you rather have a seat at the table in collaboration? I am hoping the answer is obvious. When you understand this, you realize the most powerful prayer position is seated in heavenly places with Christ. It has nothing to do with whether you are on your knees, on your face, or sitting on your behind; none of that has anything to do with Kingdom prayer. Kingdom prayer places the onus on God. The responsibility, liability, burden of proof, and obligation is on God, not you. You get to partner with God and work with Him like it says in the beginning of 2 Corinthians 6:1.

You have the power and authority to bring the atmosphere of Heaven wherever God tells you to bring it, and *because* the Kingdom is within, you can then manifest the Kingdom of Heaven *wherever* you go. YES! When you begin to see yourself as a co-creator and collaborator with God about what needs to happen in your world and how to bring it, nothing on Earth can stop you.

When I was an early teen, I secretly wanted to be an actress. I always loved television and film and was fascinated by how the people on the screens could portray emotion even though they knew exactly what everyone else was about to say. I loved the creativity and delivery of acting. But I grew up in a religious setting that basically said going to Hollywood was like going into hell itself. The general consensus was that "acting" wasn't of God and that Hollywood would corrupt you. I feared that any good virtue I possessed would be gone, snatched, taken away, worse, forfeited. With proper coaching/training, I knew I could act, and I knew the boundaries I would try to uphold. But in the back of my mind, I questioned my motives for wanting to be on "hell-a-vision" in modern day "Sodom and Gomorrah." I was so conflicted and concluded that I could not serve God and be an actress. It was not possible to do both, so I abandoned the desire.

Traditional religious settings taught that certain things were the world's and thus we should stay away. But just because something has been hijacked and used improperly doesn't mean God didn't have an original reason and purpose for it. In fact, how can it be rescued or redeemed if the people designed to do so stay away? Binoculars can be used by bird watchers or peeping toms. The binoculars aren't inherently bad. They have a purpose, and that purpose can be used for ill or for good. My hope is that this book brings freedom to you and gets you excited about prayer from God's viewpoint.

> *"All things were made through Him, and without Him nothing was made that was made."* (John 1:3 NKJV)

> *"Christ is the visible image of the invisible God. He existed before anything was created and is supreme over all creation, for through him God created everything in the heavenly realms and on earth. He made the things we can see and the things we can't see—such as thrones, Kingdoms, rulers, and authorities in the unseen world.* **Everything was created through him and for him***.*" (Colossians 1:15-16 NLT)

Remember, reason reflects the heart of the creator; purpose reflects the function of the creation.

CONNECTION

Prayer was not invented by man. It was invented by God. If it was God's idea, then like anything that belongs to God or was created by God, it has a function in the Kingdom and displays the heart of God. Since Jesus is supreme over all creation and everything was created in Him, it is fitting that Jesus teaches us how to pray. I'll go more into that in the next chapter. Since God created prayer, Kingdom prayer is about connection, co-creation, and conquering.

What is His reason? **The reason prayer exists is for connection with mankind through communication.** When I say connection, I don't just mean mechanics, I mean intimate personal linkage. God created prayer to connect through communication with man. To further illustrate this point, I need to use the French language. I love French and studied it for many years. On my first vacation to Paris, I had an open vision in my 35 square meter studio Airbnb overlooking the Eiffel Tower. I saw a French verb in white letters against a black background. The word was *CONNAÎTRE*. The word means to know. But it is different from the French verb word SAVOIR, which also means to know. *Savoir* connotes knowledge of something or about something. Millions of people can say they know (*savoir*) Oprah. Connaître connotes personal acquaintance or intimate knowledge of someone or something. Not many can say they know Oprah personally or intimately know (*connaître*) Oprah.

As mentioned in this book's important foundation section, the heart of God is family. He wants a connection with you. He desires ongoing communication with you. He wants a *relationship* with you. That is the reason prayer exists—to reflect God's heart for a connected relationship.

Prayer was designed to demonstrate and deepen our connection with God. Genesis 1:26 (NKJV) gives us a peek into the *relational conversation that produced the first prayer*. In connection and conversation with each other, the Trinity began to create on Earth.

What was the first prayer between God and man? It's in Genesis 3:8-9 (NKJV). After the fall, Adam and Eve's eyes were opened, and they sewed fig leaves together to hide their nakedness.

> *And they heard the sound of the Lord God walking in the garden in the cool of the day, and Adam and his wife hid themselves from the presence of the Lord God among the trees of the garden. Then the Lord God called to Adam and said to him, "Where are you?"*

Though this is the first time we see dialogue in these verses, it shows that the practice was already in place. The scripture implies that the man and the woman had *regular communication* with God. They heard the sound of the Lord. How did they know what that sounded like? Because they had a relationship with Him, they knew what He sounded like. They knew Him. In French, you'd say *Ils le connaissaient.* They knew that He would come for them because He did so before. Though we aren't privy to what the exact words are, we can see that before the fall, communication between God and mankind was intimate and free flowing. There are no magic words in prayer. The point is that regardless of the time, there is *regular* time spent connecting with God.

Someone who does not know God can still cry out to Him, and He answers. Religion wants you to think that if you are not performing perfectly, God does not hear you. How then would anyone become born again? Many of us have a Google, Alexa, or Siri device that low key listens out for our voice. If we say, "Hey Google," the device activates. To respond to us, there must be a low level of listening the device does. If, while we were sinners, Christ died for us, that means there is always some level of connection God has with every human being on Earth. God alone knows the hearts of man, and He is always seeking us. This is the goodness of God. God is, always has been, and always will be good!

CO-CREATION: CLIMATES AND ATMOSPHERES

Kingdom prayer is about connection, co-creation, and conquering. Connection is important because that's where you can begin to understand the heart and intention of the Father. Let's talk about co-creation because this brings us to the purpose of prayer. Have you ever wondered what the first prayer in the Bible was? When I asked, Holy Spirit showed me that the first prayer ever prayed was in Genesis 1:3 (NKJV): *Then God said, "Let there be light"; and there was light.* I didn't understand how that was the first prayer ever prayed. It certainly did not sound like prayer to me. That's when God started teaching me about the purpose of prayer.

In fact, this "first prayer" demonstrates the purpose of prayer. "Let there be light…" were the first words uttered by God to Earth in the act of creation. Did you notice the first prayer was said regarding Earth? I submit to you that prayer was specifically created for Earth. If prayer was specifically created for Earth, then in the beginning, God is demonstrating what it was supposed to be used for. **The purpose of prayer is to create atmospheres that usher and sustain the climate of Heaven, specifically Third Heaven.** Prayer is for recreating what is in Heaven here. Prayer is not needed in Third Heaven because everything already perfectly exists there as God wants. Prayer is for Earth. The function of prayer is to co-create with God on Earth whatever is already in Heaven. This explains why the first prayer to Earth was creative in nature.

As I was studying Kingdom prayer from a reason and purpose viewpoint and when He asked me to teach it, He said, "Julia, prayer is the legislative language of kings in the Kingdom. It is the language that teaches my king-priest kids how to govern the areas over which I have given them dominion." And it all started in the garden with Adam. Before the fall, man didn't have to toil the ground. He could just speak to the earth and what he spoke happened. Why? Because Adam and Eve employed prayer according to its God-created, God-invented function. Adam was mentored and tutored by God. Genesis 2:19 talks about God bringing all the animals to Adam to see what he would call them. "Call" in the Hebrew translation means to read, cry out, proclaim. Adam was practicing his authority. He was being taught how to govern the areas over which he had authority.

As we covered in our foundations, the Kingdom is a government. It has a ruler, a way to rule, and a territory to rule over. Let's build on that foundation and apply it to how God created Earth to run by talking about atmospheres and climates.

Everything on Earth is subject to the atmosphere. An atmosphere is the pervading tone or mood of a place, situation, or work of art. A climate is the condition prevailing in an area over a long period. Climates are atmospheres sustained over time.

If you go to the desert, you'll find a desert climate because an arid atmosphere has been sustained for a long period. The climate of the desert has taken on its atmosphere over time. The area near the equator is humid and hot because it has sustained that atmosphere over time.

If the purpose of prayer is to create atmospheres that usher and sustain the climate of Third Heaven, then let's quickly break down 1st, 2nd, and 3rd Heaven. Refer to Figure 2.

HEAVENLY INFLUENCE ON EARTH

<u>3rd Heaven</u>
Realm of God
This realm exists outside of creation and is used to describe God's dwelling and where Jesus reigns.
Think: this is where you spiritually existed before you got to earth. All things pertaining to life and godliness (2 Pet 1:3) originate here.

<u>2nd Heaven</u>
Realm of the invisible supernatural
Think: the realm of angels, power and principalities, etc.

<u>1st Heaven</u>
Realm of the invisible natural
Think: layers of earth's atmospheres.

EARTH

First Heaven is the invisible natural

When God created the earth, He created the territory and the atmosphere on Earth. First Heaven is what is called the *invisible natural*. There are the natural things that exist that we cannot see such as the troposphere, stratosphere, mesosphere, thermosphere, and exosphere. We do not see atmospheres; they are invisible, but they are natural, and they play a part in what is happening on the territory. Our atmosphere and climates dictate weather.

Second Heaven is the invisible supernatural.

Second Heaven is the *invisible supernatural*. This is the realm of angels and demons, the realm where the supernatural exists. When we talk about powers, principalities, rulers of the air, or spiritual wickedness in high places, we are referring to Second Heaven, the invisible supernatural. When the scriptures talk about Satan being the prince of the air, the air was Second Heaven. There is a supernatural world living among us right now. Second Heaven can and does infiltrate First Heaven and Earth. We see this when the angel told Daniel that he was held up in the heavens for 21 days. We see it in Jacob's dream of a ladder where angels were ascending and descending. All the invisible supernatural *can* actually come into the invisible natural. We do not see it because it is invisible, but at times the invisible becomes visible, and it is possible to see angels and demons. We see where angels physically appeared and walked and talked to people. Angels are the army of God. If you look at Heaven as a government of the Kingdom, the angels are the national defense. Not only do they defend, but they also play the offensive: *"So shall My word be that goes forth from My mouth; It shall not return to Me void,"* (Isaiah 55:11 NKJV). He has angels assigned and connected to what He desires to do on the earth.

Third Heaven is God's dominion dimension.

Third Heaven is God's dominion dimension. This is where God has chosen to manifest Himself. God is eternal. He does not fit into Third Heaven, Third Heaven emanates from Him. It's not like Heaven is God's house because nothing can contain Him. He created Third Heaven and chose to manifest all His glory there. When the Bible speaks about angels coming to and fro before the throne of God, it is talking about Third

Heaven. In Third Heaven, there is no weeping; there are no tears, there is no pain, and everything is in perfect unison. When God says He's given us all things pertaining to life and godliness, they exist in Third Heaven. Know that when Jesus says, "On Earth as it is in Heaven", He is referring to Third Heaven. This is why prayer is for the earth and not Third Heaven. There is nothing that needs to be created that isn't already there. Third Heaven is the dimension of God's domain and the origin point of His governing system. It's coming from Third Heaven. Why is this important when it comes to prayer?

THE BATTLE IS FOR AGREEMENT

The real battle is for agreement. In superhero movies, the fight is not over who is most powerful. The fight is about who will have the influence. In *Avengers: Infinity War*, the battle between the Avengers and Thanos was not about who was more powerful. It was about who would get to exert their governing system, their way, their impact over the world. If Thanos did, then he was going to snap his fingers and eliminate half the world population. If the Avengers did, they were going to leave things be.

If the battle is for agreement, whose agreement do spiritual forces need? Yours. They battle for your agreement because God said, *"Let Us make man, and he would have dominion over this place called Earth"* (Genesis 1:26). God's desire was for the human race to have dominion over Earth. With whomever a person agrees, that is the atmosphere that can be sustained. If you agree with God, then you come into alignment with what God wants to do—His way of governing and His way of seeing justice fulfilled. That battle for agreement happens in Second Heaven. What God said is forever already established in Third Heaven. Nothing is changing it. But it can change on Earth based on man's agreement. Since Second Heaven can infiltrate First Heaven, whatever is taking place in the heavenly atmosphere directly affects what is taking place on Earth.

When you agree with Heaven, you can then turn around and speak with authority and power into the territory He has given you dominion over and say, "This is what God says, so come forth."

What is the atmosphere of Heaven? The scripture states, *"The Kingdom of God is righteousness, peace, and joy in the Holy Spirit"* (Romans 14:17). That is what you can expect when the Kingdom of God is present.

Prayer is the conduit for co-creation with God

Every good gift and every perfect gift is from above, and comes down from the Father of lights, with whom there is no variation or shadow of turning. (James 1:17 NKJV)

Everything that God has said about you—your business, your family, your health, your wealth, what you are called to do, and your function—is in perfect form, and exists in multiple ways in the vastness of God's dimension. Since we understand that the Kingdom is the extension of God's ways of doing things from Third Heaven into Earth *through us*, we must ask, how does it get to Earth? What is the conduit? *It is prayer.* Prayer is the conduit by which man co-creates with God.

The reason for prayer is to reflect the heart of the Creator to connect continually with you. The purpose of something's existence is to reflect the function of the creation. Prayer is about creating an atmosphere that brings Third Heaven to wherever you are in the territory of Earth. The atmosphere of Heaven is love, joy, peace, patience, meekness, gentleness, kindness, and self-control. All the answers you seek exist in God's dimension of Third Heaven, and it is your duty and calling to bring forth those things and see them manifest in the earth.

Prayer is also a conduit for the expansion of the Kingdom of God. Remember from our foundation that God created a family and a government and wanted to expand both. The increase of his government shall have no end. It creates the atmosphere of Heaven wherever you are. Whatever you need, there is no lack in Heaven. If you need wisdom, *"Let him ask of God, who gives to all liberally and without reproach, and it will be given to him"* (James 1:5 NKJV). Why? Where is perfect wisdom? Where is the answer to every question that you will ever have? The answer to every question that you have is already found in Christ because all things were created in Him and for Him. Prayer brings the atmosphere of Heaven, so that the *climate* of Heaven can be established here on Earth through your business, family, customers, customer service, marketing, product development, research development, and your partnerships.

Myles Munroe said this, *"Prayer is the most important and the most misunderstood key in the Kingdom because prayer unlocks all the other doors."*[6] You and I know that the prayer meeting at any church or at any place is the least attended event. Matthew 16:19 states, *"And I will give you the keys of the Kingdom of heaven"* (NKJV). There are many keys to the Kingdom of Heaven—keys to finances, health, family, business, and your reach into the world.

Because you have access to the keys, the Bible continues in Matthew 16:19, *"And whatever you bind on Earth will be bound in Heaven. And whatever you loose on Earth will be loosed in Heaven"* (NKJV). If prayer is *the* most important key because it unlocks all the other doors, then I can agree with Heaven and show my agreement by saying, for example, "let there be health," and expect it to come forth. If I come into agreement with doubt, fear, or sickness, then the perfect shalom of Heaven will not come because I lent my authority and then my voice to agree with something that wasn't in Heaven, thereby closing the door to the partnership of Heaven.

Imagine you walk up to a two-story home where you have a room, but you only have the key to your room, not the key to the front door. How are you going to get in? When we live a life of prayerlessness, we are

---

[6] (Munroe 2013)

actually putting ourselves in a position where we have to jimmy a lock or see if a window is open that we can crawl through. When we live a life of prayerlessness, we make it harder for us to receive all God has for us because we do not know what could be possible in partnership with Him. We do not know that we have access to the power that He has. He is the key to the front door, the master key that unlocks all the other doors. What if you insert the key to prayer and all the doors in the house open to you? Now you have free reign! That is what prayer is in the Kingdom; it is creating the atmosphere so that the climate of Heaven is sustained here on Earth.

When religion says Hollywood or Corporations are dark, all we're really witnessing is it operating under its current climate. Are we seeing the darkness because the family of God did not take their places and start calling forth the atmosphere of Heaven in those territories? Man agreed with the system of darkness; therefore, the atmosphere of the system of darkness was allowed to infiltrate that territory. As Kingdom people, we're in the business of climate change.

The connection part of Kingdom Prayer is the way you get to know the Father, what He wants, and how He thinks. The co-creation part of Kingdom is where you use your agreement to grant Him permission to show up in any situation. So many people try to just name things, then claim them without partnership with Heaven and without a connection to the Father for either a *reason* or a *purpose* for what they desire.

Jesus knew that the heart of the Father was to expand the government of Heaven through the family. He had to position Himself, and keep Himself in position, so there could be more family. That is why, when we were still sinners, Christ died for us so that we could become part of the family because expansion was a family operation.

At this point, people you may be wondering about prayers of deliverance, healing, warfare, or intercessory prayers. I'll touch on those in the next chapter where I present a Kingdom framework for prayer. It's coming.

CONQUERING

As stated before, Kingdom Prayer is about connection, co-creation, and conquering. Let's dive into the conquering part. In Genesis 1:28, God said to them, *"Be fruitful and multiply; fill the earth and **subdue** it; have dominion over the fish of the sea, over the birds of the air, and over every living thing that moves on the earth."* The word subdue there comes from the Hebrew word *kāḇaš*. It means to make subservient, to subjugate, and to keep under. It implies that if something gets out of order, you can put it back in order. Romans 8:19 says all creation waits for the revealing of the sons of God. Why are they waiting on the sons of God? I heard Myron Golden say once that God made creators, creatures, and creation. Creations can only be made by creators. Since man is made in God's image, it is the only thing on Earth that has creative power. Creation knows that it is subjected to mankind and is waiting for us to realize so we can redeem it from the curse. Romans 8:20-21 ESV says

> *For the creation was subjected to futility,*
> *not willingly, but because of Him who subjected it in hope;*
> *because the creation itself also will be delivered*
> *from the bondage of corruption*
> *into the glorious liberty of the children of God.*

The Amplified Bible translates verse 21 this way:

> *that the creation itself*
> *will also **be freed from its bondage to decay***
> *[and gain entrance] into*
> *the glorious freedom of the children of God.*

This verse indicates that creation is in bondage and is waiting to be freed. Could it be that just as Jesus was The Messiah for humanity on Earth, humanity is the messiah for creation on Earth? Before you clutch your pearls, just hang on a second. The way God set it up, Earth is the place of man's rule and creation to be dominated and subdued by man. The scriptures say, just as Adam allowed the curse to enter the earth because of sin, Jesus, the last Adam, returned everything back to its original order. The work of the cross was not to change God's mind about you. It was to change your mind about God. With a right view of God, you have a right view of everything God created, including yourself and all creation. Therefore, I submit to you that creation is waiting for Kingdom sons and daughters to free it. This begs many questions. But I'll start with this one: what is the process of freeing creation called? It is called conquering! It is redeeming creation back to its original reason and purposes. Another very good question is this: what are you to rule and have dominion over? In the next chapter, I talk about the hows, but before I do, I need to talk about you for a minute.

YOU MATTER MORE THAN YOU REALIZE

Up until this point, I have referred to man, mankind, humanity, etc. as a whole. But I want to talk about you specifically for a minute. I don't know if anyone has ever told you this, but you matter to God. Your opinions matter to God. Your interests matter to God. In fact, your interests are what God uses to expand the Kingdom. He is either using your interest to co-create or to conquer. Let me prove it to you with very familiar passages of scripture concerning the Great Commission.

Jesus tells the disciple in Matthew 28:19 to go make disciples of all nations. "Nation" in Greek is *ethnos*, where we get our English word ethnic from. We've taken this to mean all different types of ethnic people groups. This correct understanding of this version of this meaning has fueled missionary work forever. But there is another meaning to this word. It means a multitude of people of the same nature. At first glance, you'd probably say it is the same thing. But if you are a fan of the Golden State Warriors basketball team, and I say "Warrior Nation," or if you are a fan of the Pittsburgh Steelers, and I say "Steeler Nation," you'd know what I mean. Nation is used to describe a multitude of people of the same nature. What is that nature? Fanaticism for Golden State basketball or Pittsburgh football. If God is about expanding His family, that is the reason Jesus told the disciples to make disciples of all nations. Then how many nations are out there, and how do *you* know which nation is yours to disciple? To answer that question, let's go to The Book of Acts 1:8. While the Great Commission was given after the death, burial, and resurrection of Jesus, the power to fulfill the Commission came after Jesus ascended into Heaven. In Acts 1:8, Jesus said, *"But you shall receive power when the Holy Spirit has come upon you; and you shall be witnesses to Me in Jerusalem, and in all Judea and Samaria, and to the end of the earth."*

I was taught to think of Jerusalem, Judea, Samaria, and the ends of the earth like concentric circles. Begin with the people closest to you, then spread out from there. There is merit to that but there is another way to look at it too. That perspective can be found in the meaning of the city names. Jerusalem is often translated as peace. Peace is shalom. Shalom indicates a wholeness because nothing is missing or broken. Judea has been translated to mean praise. But with Hebraic words, sometimes the definition is derived from a word picture that better describes the meaning. The picture from which we get praise is the idea of throwing one's hands up or pointing as in delight, wonder and admiration. If you've ever seen someone throw up their hands at the sight of something beautiful and exciting, you know what I mean. I do it with food all the time. A good looking and good tasting dish will have my hands clapping and my fingers pointing for sure. The action of pointing to something or throwing your hands up at something that brings wonder or delight is where we get the translation praise. Samaria means guardianship. It implies one who takes great care of something. The good Samaritan story was about a person from Samaria who took great care of someone they didn't know. Let's put it all together now.

> *You shall be witnesses to me bringing wholeness (Jerusalem) to a place that delights you (Judea) as its careful guardian (Samaria).*

My doctor friend takes great delight in science. She points to medicine, the place that delights her, and trained to be its careful guardian. In the upcoming chapter about business, I talk more about the different kinds of businesses people started simply because it interested them. This is why I say your opinions and interests matter. Because if you are interested in gaming, then you get to call that creation into the wholeness of Jesus. If you are interested in knitting, animals, history, chess, politics, engineering, cars, movies, music, singing, sign language, dancing, hair styling, fashion, telecommunication, avionics… whatever you are interested in, you get to either co-create with God or conquer it—subdue or make subservient to the lordship of Jesus through you.

Because of your connected relationship with Him, He will tell you what His thoughts and intentions are about the thing. It is this reason why the Bible doesn't talk about every possible creation known to man. If expansion is on God's mind, then He uses our interests and desires as indicators of where to take God next. Take for instance George Washington Carver, an African American scientist, inventor and agriculturalist, who said "Anything will give up its secrets to you if you love it enough." In regular conversation with God, Carver asked God why He made the peanut. God's answer allowed Carver to invent hundreds of uses for the peanut that we all benefit from to this day. All because he was interested in it and God used his interest as a doorway for kingdom expansion. I wrote this book for businesspeople because business is my interest and sphere of influence. Everything I am saying so far can be applied to anyone. For my businesspeople, especially you founder CEOs, the act of going into business was an act of collaborating with God about what He wants to see happen in the world and in the marketplace. People need what you carry in business.

When you know you were made to co-create and conquer, you stop complaining about what you lack and begin to partner with God for the solutions. Slaves complain about what the master is not giving them. Sons walk about in the house, open the refrigerator, and take what they need. You are no longer a victim to the schemes and plans of the devil because you know the Greater One lives inside of you; the One who created *all* the galaxies has taken up residence on the inside of you. *"Greater is He that is in me than he who is in the world"* (1 John 4:4 KJV). What world is He talking about? He is talking about the Second Heaven realm where that authority is fought for. Authority on Earth is either abdicated or unclaimed.

You are not a victim. There are no victims in the Kingdom. There are no minorities in the Kingdom. When you come into this Kingdom with understanding, you realize that victimhood is not an identity. Victim was an incident, and Jesus has a way to work through any incidents to redeem you to the fullness of life. "*To us all things that pertain unto life and godliness*" (2 Peter 1:3 NKJV). I am not discounting anyone's traumatic experience, for I have been through some myself, but the Greater One lives inside of you.

With this understanding of the reason and purpose of prayer, and that you matter, prayer ceases to be just a spiritual discipline that we have to do. Prayer now is an exciting act of connection, co-creation, and calling those things that are not as they are with the One who created them. So get excited about partnering with your family to expand the family government in business.

Pray the Kingdom Way Prayer Prompt #1: *In this section, I talked about the reason and purpose of prayer. ASK God: What is something I currently believe about prayer that You want to change my mind about?*

CHAPTER 2

THE KINGDOM PRAYER FRAMEWORK

Now that we've established that prayer was God-made, not man-made, and that God created prayer for connection through communication with man, His son/daughters and Kingdom expanders on Earth, and to co-create the climates of Heaven on Earth, let's dive into the Kingdom Prayer Framework. There is a revival of prayer happening on the earth. More people are going to be talking about the importance of prayer for what God's doing on the earth. My goal is to help people pray more confidently. Confidence comes with experience and knowledge. Instead of making prayer MORE complicated, God wants to return us back to the simplicity of what He created. Kingdom prayer is not about magic words. It is not about formulas. Kingdom prayer is relational in nature and governmental in function. It was designed to foster deeper relationship because the reason for prayer is connection. The more you experience God, the more confident you grow in the things of God. Since Kingdom prayer is relational in nature, it ought not be formulaic in practice. I do not know about you, but this works-based prayer that has dominated most of my life, and probably most of yours as well, has too many people questioning if they are praying correctly. *What prayer do I pray today? Do I enter His gates with thanksgiving, or should I confess my sins first? Maybe I should worship first? Do I call him Father God or Daddy? Maybe I should call Him Jehovah? Wait... if I call Him Jehovah, which Jehovah do I call Him? Do I call Him Jehovah-Nissi? Do I call Him*

Jehovah-Rapha? Do I call Him Elo-Him? Do I call Him Yeshua? It was exhausting. My hope is that this framework brings simplicity and fun so you use it all the time.

FRAMEWORK VS MODEL

Before we dive into the framework, let's define some terms. In this section, I use model and framework very distinctly. A *model* is a specific system or structure used as an example to follow or imitate. Think of model car sets. The model car is a much smaller imitation of the original version. Most of the time, models are to be replicated and followed exactly as is. Think of it as a blueprint. A model can be seen as a blueprint to be followed exactly to produce the outcome. A *framework* can be viewed as a design approach. It outlines the concepts and considerations from which a design is created. A framework in general shows the relationship between concepts. A framework shows how something is connected. A model is a specific example of that connection.

Minimalism, for example, as a framework shows the relationship between the use of voids or negative space, the elimination of distractions, and the use of repetition throughout a design. Minimalist designs can be seen in art, graphic design, architecture, interior design, fashion, automotive design and even stationary. The number of examples or models of minimalist design are countless because when you understand the framework, it can be applied in an infinite number of ways.

I liken frameworks to scaffolding. On a construction project, the scaffold is a temporary and secure place for workers to access greater heights. A scaffold provides safety, position, support, and access. Safety because it provides a boundary from which to securely operate. Proper position because it puts the workers in the proper position to build or work. Support because it provides a place not just for the worker, but also for all building material needed to do the job. And finally, access because it elevates the worker to heights necessary to see, inspect, and reexamine the work. Scaffolding doesn't remain once the building is built. It is there to help build, to bring understanding, and to support the final vision. A model provides an environment to implement a framework. Don't miss that. A model is an example of how a framework can be implemented. A framework is larger than a model. Given these distinctions, it stands to reason that one framework can have many different models to illustrate its uses.

What does this have to do with prayer? As we've discussed, prayer was created by God for mankind on Earth. His reason was connection through communication. His purpose was to create atmospheres that usher and sustain the climate of Heaven on Earth. Why? Because God's whole agenda is to create a family, to bring a government and to expand both. Prayer is the conduit of connection, co-creation, and conquering.

The Framework

In the preface, I told you the context in which God asked to teach me prayer. My lane is business, supporting business, and specifically helping to advance the leaders of Kingdom business. Businesspeople wanted to pray "more" but they seemed to be stumped on how to do it without spending hours. Let me be clear, there is nothing inherently wrong with spending hours in prayer. Nothing. But if *all* you know how to do is spend hours, then it's time to expand your tool kit and learn something else. It seemed that prayer had become too convoluted. There are so many models out there, so how does one know which to employ at any given time? And so many of them are taught as steps, so what if you forget the steps? I had so many books and pamphlets earmarked and "Post-it noted" in my prayer time just in case. Until Holy Spirit said, "Let me help you." And He showed me that there is a Kingdom Prayer Framework from which all the famous prayers of the Bible, including the ones Jesus prayed, followed. It is this framework that allows for the flow and flexibility of God to connect with us and continue to usher and create the climate of Heaven on Earth in anyone, anywhere, at any time.

I call it the Kingdom Prayer Framework or TALK ◆ ASK ◆ LISTEN™ for short. See Figure 3.

Let's give an overview of the framework, then dive deep. *TALK* to God about what's on your mind. *ASK* questions to get His perspective. *LISTEN* to what He says. *DECLARE* the WHO of Him in that situation and/or the WHO of you in that situation. *DECREE* what He says to say. That's it. Every prayer known or spoken on Earth uses at least one part of the framework.

TALK

Talking is the easiest part of prayer. It is where we pour out our heart, words, feelings, opinions, scriptures etc. to God. We monologue about whatever is on our mind. That is not a bad thing. It's biblical to do so. The scriptures clearly tell us to cast all our cares on the Lord (1 Peter 5:7). We are to come to Jesus if we're burdened to find rest (Matthew 11:28). We're also told to reason with God in Isaiah 1:18. Hebrew 4:16 tells us to come boldly. In fact, we're instructed over and over again to come to God and keep coming to God. Why? Because connection is on His mind. God loves when you talk to Him about anything and everything. *Well, Julia, doesn't He already know what I'm going to say? How I feel?* He does. In the 2017 movie *The Shack,* Mac sat talking at the dinner table with the Trinity and made the same point. To which Sarayu, the Holy Spirit character, says "Yes. We choose to listen to everything you have to say as if it was the first time." If you are a parent, or have been around children, you can understand this point. You've heard their favorite story a million times, but each time they tell it to you, even though you know exactly what they are going to say, you listen and engage with them. Why? The point isn't the content. The point is the connection. By listening to them, they feel seen and loved. They bond with you and trust you. In the garden, God regularly spoke to them, not to convince Himself of their usefulness, but to show them His character so they would trust Him. Remember, what you believe about God determines how you'll interact with Him. So you have to get to know Him, and you can only get to know someone better through communication. He communicates to you through the scriptures and through personal experience. This is why I said that you have to settle on two important truths: God is GOOD and God is LOVE. It is easy to talk to someone you know loves you and is good to you. The things you talk to Him about are always doing two things. One: It is Deepening your relationship with Him and making Him more real to you. Two: Expanding His Kingdom on Earth. The first thing is self-explanatory. He wants you to get to know Him better.

But may you ask, how is it expanding the Kingdom? As mentioned in the section about making disciples in Jerusalem, Judea, Samaria and the ends of the earth, the things that matter to you matter to Him. The things that delight you or upset you are always areas that can bring the climate of Heaven to that situation, even if the only beneficiary is you. Religion taught me that I shouldn't bother God with "small stuff." It implied that He was too important, too busy keeping the galaxy running to be bothered with something so small as my unrequited teenage crush asking another girl to the prom. Or that I struggled with my multiplication facts. So I decided to only go to Him for the "big stuff." This is where the accuser got me. He would say, *"Don't take that to God. It's not important enough."* Then when I wanted to bring an "important" thing to Him, the accuser would say, *"You only come to God when you want something."* Or *"You haven't talked to Him all week/month/year and now you expect He'll listen and answer."* Then I didn't know that I could only go to God when I needed something even if I hadn't communicated with Him in a while. He designed prayer for connection, so He always wants to hear from me. It's in the conversation about cars, planes, and video games that I show my children that I care about them so that they come to me with anything. It happens while talking. You can go to God about ANYTHING small or large because it's all small to Him. When my oldest son was in third grade, math was very hard for him. He was preparing for a test on a unit that was particularly difficult. We encouraged him to ask God for help and we prayed. He took the test and came home with a good grade. "God helped me," he said. My heart just burst open. The look on his face was pure joy that God took time to help him with third grade math. He saw then and there that he mattered to God. He learned that his existence mattered to God, not just his deeds. Catch that. From that point on, it became an inside joke between me and my husband. We say, "It's all third grade math," to remind us that it's all small stuff to God.

Let me talk to you businesspeople for a minute. Your business matters to God. I know so many business people who are hesitant to talk to God about business because of erroneous thoughts and accusations. You don't have to give half your revenue to missions, put a scripture on your products, sponsor a village, build a school, or have Bible study in your office before you can talk to God about the situations, especially the financial situations, in your business. You can talk to Him about anything.

Up until this point, the TALK part has been about you initiating conversation with God. But as you know from personal experience, and from what is shown in the Bible, God initiates conversation with us, too. Know that TALK can be initiated by either party at any time. If you've ever been awakened in the wee hours of the morning, you know this. The most secure relationships you have are the ones that are reciprocal. Your closest friends call you. You aren't always the ones doing the calling, right? The TALK part of the framework is about connection through conversation, regardless of topic or initiator.

ASK

The ASK part of the framework is not just you asking if God will do this or that. The ASK part is about you asking God for His perspective on what you talked to Him about. Romans 12:2 tells us that all transformation begins in the mind. I like how the New Living Translation puts it:

> *Don't copy the behavior and customs of this world, but let God transform you into a new person by changing the way you think. Then you will learn to know God's will for you, which is good and pleasing and perfect.*

How do you renew your mind? How do we let God change the way we think? How do you learn what God wants, likes, and desires? When you are bogged down under the weight of your thoughts, opinions, and feelings on something, how do you begin to make the exchange? You already know what you think and feel about a situation. What you either don't know or lack confidence in is what God thinks. You know how you feel about the business, the politician, the person, or the situation. But have you asked God what He thinks about the business, politician, person, or situation? In my religious upbringing, I was told that you don't question God. I, like most of us, took it to mean that it was disrespectful and irreverent to ask God any question at all. But that doesn't line up with the scriptures. Jesus told us to ask, seek, and knock in Matthew 7:7 and Luke 11:9. If we lack wisdom, we're to ask of the Lord. We're even told that we don't have it because we didn't ask (James 4:2). So if it's ok to ask God, then ask God. The ASK part of prayer is when you invite God to change your mind on a topic if it needs to be changed or to confirm His perspective so you grow in faith. In the APPENDIX section of this book, I offer over 125 ASK PROMPTS to give you cool questions to jump start your conversation with God. It is not to be used religiously but as a catalyst to your own conversation. ASK prompt questions are as simple and direct as, "God, what do you think about this?" My favorite ones are more pointed. One such question is, "What perspective do you have that I need?" Remember, if the purpose of prayer is to usher and sustain the climate of Heaven, wouldn't it make sense to know as much as possible about what Heaven says? When we don't ask, we guess, or we presume. The process of asking fortifies your confidence, your trust, and your faith. I did a prayer challenge for business owners for which the subtitle was "How to pray profits into your business without manipulating God, fighting the devil, and spending hours on your knees." Too many of us are in the habit of praying from our perspective and not Heaven's. Because of that, it can be hard to know if we're manipulating God or praying illegal prayers. But you cannot manipulate God when you partnered with Him to create the very prayer you prayed.

LISTEN

The LISTEN part of the framework is my favorite, even though it was the hardest part for me at first. When I say *listen*, it is easy to assume that I mean using your ears. It implies that you should expect to hear God audibly through your ears. This is not the case. I use *listen* to indicate how you recognize what you receive from Him. You can *listen* to Him and see a picture, feel a feeling, hear something, or just know it. You can *listen* to Him through scripture, lyrics, dreams, visitations, or through movie lines. God is a master communicator and knows how to "speak" to all of creation, especially you. The wind had no ears, yet it listened and obeyed the voice of Jesus and calmed down. Listening is about identifying and valuing ALL the ways you hear from God. What I love about the new testament prophetic teaching/ training out now is that it focuses on the myriad of ways you can "hear" God. If you think you can only hear God audibly with your ears, that is the only way you are going to be open to hearing Him. For people who tell me they have a hard time listening, in most cases, it is a recognition issue. They are not recognizing how God is already speaking to them or they aren't honoring it. God speaks to me through movie lines and song lyrics and no, not all of the movies or songs are "Christian." I grew up in the nineties and was familiar with hip hop music. Any hip hop song I knew, I knew because it came on the radio at my cousin's house. A few years back, when I was in the throes of developing my prophetic gifting, out of the blue, I heard Craig Mack's lyrics in my head. *Here comes a brand new flava in your ear. Time for new flava in your ear. I'm kickin' new flava in your ear.* It was on repeat in my head. This wasn't the first time that happened. God is a master communicator and He used those lyrics to signal a shift in my prophetic hearing. I could look back throughout my life and see random songs popping in my head. It was God speaking to me and me listening. A lyric can be a catalyst for conversation IF you use it to ASK. Sometimes God's voice sounds just like you. What most of us do when we perceive something is dismiss it in favor of our preferred style. My primary way of hearing God is by feeling. When I feel something, I tune in and then I wait for the words. I've grown in listening because I practiced it. When I was in college, I wanted to speak in tongues so bad. Someone gave me a booklet about it, and at the end it had a prayer to ask for the gift. I will never forget it.

I was on my knees beside my bed in my dorm room. I prayed the prayer and waited. The book said that I would hear something and to say what I heard. I waited. And waited. And waited. I was determined. When my mind would wonder about a class or something, I'd bring it back and just listen. Then it happened. I heard a syllable in my head. It wasn't a language. It was just a syllable. *Ok, Julia,* I encouraged myself, *Just say what you heard.* So I did. It sounded more like the bleating of sheep than the boisterous and fluent tongues I heard at church. It was something like *ba ba*. Guess who showed up in my head at that point? The devil. He was like, *That ain't it. You know you look and sound real stupid right now, right?* But if I could hear and recognize when the enemy spoke to me, the scripture said that His sheep know His voice, so I guess it was fitting that those first words I heard sounded like sheep. I kept going and repeated what I heard again and again until I heard something else. That is how I got "baptized in the Holy Ghost with the evidence of speaking in tongues." It was the most elementary, least charismatic experience of truth. I heard stories of how the Spirit would "fall" and suddenly everyone was speaking in rolling tongues of all kinds. I thought that would be my experience too. But it wasn't. My mind and intellect were very much involved. I kept practicing month after month until eventually, it flowed. But it all started with listening. At first, I wished God would do a spontaneous thing and BAM—out it all came. But the process of listening for Him to speak to me like that forever solidified that I could hear God. It was no longer a question of *if* I could hear. Nowadays it is more about how He wants to talk to me now. If you struggle with this question, I have a simple exercise for you. The next time the question, *"Do I hear God?"* comes up. Answer it out loud, *"Yes I hear God."* Then turn your attention to God and ask Him, what are the ways you speak to me? Better questions yield better fruit. I guarantee He'll answer you. You'll begin to recognize those ways yourself.

The LISTEN part of the framework opens you up to get insider information. Jeremiah 33: 3 tells us that God will show us things we never knew if we just call to Him. Sometimes it may take a while to hear, and other times it doesn't. In fact, when I began focusing my attention on prayer in the business setting, I challenged myself and God. I said, (TALK) *God, I need to learn to hear you faster. These business folks don't have time to be waiting for a response all night. These leaders need to know how to hear you in the moment, at the negotiation table, and in the middle of the presentation. So I want to practice hearing you faster (ASK).* That's how I grew. I had already learned to tarry, wait, and soak. I can still hear Juanita Bynum's lyrics. *I don't mind waiting. I don't mind waiting. I don't mind waiting on you Lord.* I learned that. And because I learned that, I will always have the ability to patiently wait on God. But that wasn't the skillset needed for where I was going. I needed to learn to hear God when I only had ninety seconds with a leader, so that's what we practiced.

If you'll notice in the diagram, there are continuity arrows going around to TALK ◆ ASK ◆ LISTEN™. This indicated that it is perfectly acceptable to repeat TALK ◆ ASK ◆ LISTEN™ as many times as needed. Sometimes it will be ASK ◆ LISTEN ◆ TALK. Sometimes it will be LISTEN◆TALK. The order doesn't matter. The conversation does. The more He talks to you about His perspective on the situation, you may have more questions. So you ask and listen some more. This is how something becomes revelation to you. This is how you test the spirits to see if they are from God. You bring it to Him. When I hear something preached, I have said many times to the Holy Spirit, *something doesn't feel right about what I heard or observed* (TALK). *What am I sensing?* (ASK). Then He'll confirm that I discerned correctly, or He'll tell me that I couldn't receive what was said because of a wrong mindset or issue in my heart. Remember when I said I never understood how someone can pray without ceasing? When He taught me the TALK ◆ ASK ◆ LISTEN™ part of the framework, I could easily see it. When I adopted this as my prayer foundation, I was talking to God all the time, about everything. I was praying without ceasing; it just didn't look like the hour-long prayer sessions I was used to. I TALK ◆ ASK ◆ LISTEN™ in the car, at the grocery store, at the doctor's office, in traffic, with friends, and with clients. The repetition of it creates what's called buy-in. Buy-in is defined as acceptance of or willingness to actively support and participate in something. God wants you to buy-in. Let's take a look at a very familiar passage of scripture. In Matthew 26: 36-45, Jesus is in the garden of Gethsemane praying before going to the cross.

> *"Then Jesus went with his disciples to a place called Gethsemane, and he said to them, "Sit here while I go over there and pray." 37 He took Peter and the two sons of Zebedee along with him, and he began to be sorrowful and troubled. 38 Then he said to them, "My soul is overwhelmed with sorrow to the point of death. Stay here and keep watch with me." 39 Going a little farther,* **he fell with his face to the ground and prayed**, *"My Father, if it is possible, may this cup be taken from me. Yet not as I will, but as you will." 40 Then he returned to his disciples and found them sleeping. "Couldn't you men keep watch with me for one hour?" he asked Peter. 41 "Watch and pray so that you will not fall into temptation. The spirit is willing, but the flesh is weak." 42* **He went away a second time and prayed**, *"My Father, if it is not possible for this cup to be taken away unless I drink it, may your will be done." 43 When he came back, he again found them sleeping, because their eyes were heavy. 44 So* **he left them and went away once more and prayed the third time**, *saying the same thing. 45 Then he returned to the disciples and said to them, "Are you still sleeping and resting? Look, the hour has come, and the Son of Man is delivered into the hands of sinners."* Matt 26:36-45 ESV

I grew up with the KJV version, and in it, verse 42 reads, *Saying, Father, if thou be willing, remove this cup from me: nevertheless, not my will, but thine, be done.* If I had a nickel for every sermon I heard on "nevertheless not my will but thine be done", I'd have thousands. When we read that, it is easy to think that the whole sentence was breathed in one single breath. But what if the passage showed us how Jesus used TALK ♦ ASK ♦ LISTEN™ to gain buy-in to the hardest things He ever had to face? I submit to you that He did. He entered into TALK ♦ ASK ♦ LISTEN™ a minimum of *three* times. Remember when I said I wanted to be an actress. Well, my acting skills kick in when I teach this live. I get really dramatic to illustrate the point. It's so fun and impactful. Each time He went to the Father, they talked and exchanged ideas and support about what they were about to do until it was time to proceed. Jesus wasn't the only who used TALK ♦ ASK ♦ LISTEN™. David was the king, pun intended, of pouring out his feelings to God until his feelings conformed to God's will. Make no mistake. God cares about your feelings. He just won't change His mind about His agenda because of them. Jonah, Moses, and Esther can testify to that. *We* have to change our minds. Because we have free will and have spiritual authority on the earth, it is vital that when we speak to the natural or spiritual world, we are congruent with what we're saying. TALK ♦ ASK ♦ LISTEN™ is how we get congruent. We need to exercise our faith, and faith comes by hearing and hearing by the Word of God, right? So the more you engage in TALK ♦ ASK ♦ LISTEN™, the greater your faith for what needs to be said or done.

DECLARE

Once you have TALKed ♦ ASKed ♦ LISTENed to get God's perspective, intent, and submitted to His thoughts, then you get to co-create the atmosphere shift with God and DECLARE. To declare something means to let it be known. It is to state, out loud, a fact or truth. People think declarations are decrees and they are not. They go together so it's understandable.

The DECLARE part of the framework is about acknowledging the spiritual truth of who God is or of who a person is and what they have access to because of Jesus. This part of the framework is about what truth or knowledge needs to be made known. In DECLARE, there are typically two things that need to be made known depending on the topic you're praying about: 1) the character, name or Word of God and/or 2) the character or authority of the person speaking or the subject of the prayer.

Making known the character or name of God might sound like:

> *I declare that You are Emmanuel, God with us…*
> *Let it be known that at the Name of Jesus every knee has to bow…*
> *You are Elohim, the Almighty one, the Alpha and Omega, the Author and Perfecter…*

Making known the Word of God, scripture, or promises might sound like:

> *You said in Psalm 23 that because You are my shepherd*
> *I will not want anything…*
> *According to Deuteronomy 28, You already said…*

Making known who you are as the speaker might sound like:

> *I declare that I have the mind of Christ…*
> *I arise in my authority as the executive of this business…*

The scripture says faith comes by hearing. In the DECLARE part of prayer, your faith grows because you have heard what God wants you to declare. Declarations shift spiritual atmospheres and cause them to be attentive to the authority of Christ and the Christ in you.

DECREE

Once you have TALKed ◆ ASKed ◆ LISTENed to get God's perspective, intent, and submitted to His thoughts, then you get to co-create legislation with God and DECREE. To decree something means to issue an authoritative command. This is the fun "on earth as it is in Heaven" part of prayer. Decrees have the power to shift things from a spiritual existence to the natural one. In Mark 11:14, Jesus said to the fig tree, "May no one ever eat fruit from you again." That decree changed the natural state of the tree forever. Every command Jesus gave the winds were decrees. I offer a Decree Workshop where we get together to use the Kingdom Prayer Framework to craft decrees over ourselves, our businesses, and our family. The testimonials from that workshop are amazing because the people partner with God to craft the specific declarations and decrees over certain situations. In the government of the Kingdom, decrees expand the kingdom because they reach in the micro-spaces of our human existence.

I was speaking to a friend of mine recently who hit a snag in her business that threw her for a loop. I did some TALK ◆ ASK ◆ LISTEN™ to get God's perspective. I am VERY protective of my friends, so when something hurtful happens, my emotions want to react. But when I learned this framework, I had to learn not to respond out of emotion but to seek God on what position and perspective I should take. This is important. There are times I pray from my position as *daughter* and then there are times I pray from my position as royalty and ruler. In my TALK ◆ ASK ◆ LISTEN™ to God about my friend, I calmed down enough to receive His perspective and vision. He showed me a picture of what was happening in the spirit realm (Second Heaven & Third Heaven) over her and her business. Then I asked what needed to be made known. For this situation, He said, "use the authority you have as her friend to speak to this." Then He told me what to decree, and I said what He said to command a shift to occur. The reason these two go together is because it is very easy to shift from declare to decree and vice versa.

HOW IT WORKS IN REAL TIME

Now that we've outlined the framework, it is important to note a few things:

1. NOT every prayer interaction will have all the components of the framework.
2. The parts do not always happen in the order presented.
3. You may naturally flow between the parts as you employ it more.

You don't have to say, "I declare" to make a declaration nor do you have to say, "I decree" when making a decree. Conversely, when you do say it, you build a solid foundation of confidence in prayer because you know what you're doing.

The point of the Kingdom Prayer Framework is to talk to God, ask His thoughts, release what needs to be known, and then tell stuff what to do.

Every prayer model follows at least one section of this framework.

Prayers of confession use the TALK part of the framework.

Prayers of supplication or petition use the TALK ◆ ASK ◆ LISTEN part of the framework.

Prayers of worship and adoration just use the DECLARE part of the framework.

Prayers of intercession use the entire TALK ◆ ASK ◆ LISTEN ◆ DECLARE ◆ DECREE framework.

Prayers of thanksgiving use the TALK or DECLARE part of the framework.

Prayer for healing use the whole TALK ◆ ASK ◆ LISTEN ◆ DECLARE ◆ DECREE framework.

The prayer of Jabez uses the TALK and DECREE part of the framework.

When Jesus was at Lazarus's tomb in John 11:41-44 (NIV), He used the DECLARE ◆ DECREE parts of the framework.

> *Vs 41 Then Jesus looked up and said, "Father, I thank you that you have heard me."*

This is the TALK part. He didn't say this after He told Lazarus to come out. He said it before to reiterate His connection with Father God.

> *42 "I knew that you always hear me, but I said this for the benefit of the people standing here, that they may believe that you sent me."*

This is the DECLARE part. He declared that He was sent from God and that not only does God hear Him, but all creation does too.

> *43 When he had said this, Jesus called in a loud voice, "Lazarus, come out!"*

This is a DECREE. He commanded something to happen.

Let's look at the most famous prayer in Christianity and see the framework.

Our Father in heaven,
TALK/DECLARE
Hallowed be Your name.
DECLARE
Your Kingdom come.
Your will be done

On earth as it is in heaven.
DECREE
Give us this day our daily bread.
And forgive us our debts,
As we forgive our debtors.
ASK/DECREE
And do not lead us into temptation,
But deliver us from the evil one.
DECREE
(Matthew 6:9-13 NKJV)

Jesus never meant for this model to be repeated verbatim. In fact, Jesus warned in the verses right before not to do that.

"And when you pray, do not use vain repetitions as the heathen do. For they think that they will be heard for their many words. Therefore, do not be like them. For your Father knows the things you have need of before you ask Him." (Matthew 6:7-8 NKJV).

I believe we use a lot of words in prayer because we like sounding a certain way, or to build up our faith to believe what we're praying for. I will be the first to admit that, sometimes when I pray prayers of thanksgiving, I love to use a good old-fashioned sing-song voice when I pray. The Black women who raised me taught me in that style and it's fun to me and makes me feel good. It's a style preference. The power of prayer is not in its style, delivery, or repetition of a model. It isn't in its steps. It is in its origin in Jesus Christ. Listen, when you adopt the TALK ♦ ASK ♦ LISTEN™ framework and co-create with the One who created all things, it boosts your confidence.

A few years ago, the movie *War Room* came out. Suddenly everybody and their mama went home and cleaned out a closet and made it a "war room." I'm not saying that God didn't tell some of those people to do that, but I know good and well a lot of people didn't hear God and just jumped on the bandwagon. In Christian circles we tend to amplify and repeat a model that looked or sounded good or produced a favorable outcome in another's life rather than seeking to understand the purpose for the model. This is the nature of humanity. As stated before, the nature of a framework permits a myriad of models. I am not against models. Through them the Kingdom is expanded. However, I do raise caution when models mask purpose. Models make it easier to not receive insight or specific direction from God. The Kingdom Prayer Framework will never amplify a tactic over the Sovereign. It will never exclude God from prayer. To pray the Kingdom way, you must go through the Trinity to be effective. I was asked on more than one occasion if I had a prayer closet and was frowned at when I told them no. On a humorous note, I knew better than to set myself up for that type of failure because I know me. If I get around to cleaning out a closet, it is because it needs to be cleaned out. And if I do prayer in that closet, it won't be long before I change locations because I need more space or because I get bored doing the same thing the same way for long. If that's what God told you to do, go for it. If you genuinely like it, do it. But if you think that by doing it or having it, it will increase or decrease your chances of being seen, heard, or answered, that's a problem. I am not against having a physical closet, but did we miss the point because we got so fixated on the model? The star of the movie was PRAYER, not the room. Truth be told, the person who wrote your favorite books or teachings on prayer got the revelation for those books and teaching through TALK ♦ ASK ♦ LISTEN™. They were talking to God or God was talking to them. Questions were exchanged. Listening took place and then BOOM! Now there's a book. Now there's teaching. Now there is documentation of their revelation for all posterity. This works to advance the Kingdom on Earth.

CONNECTION AND CO-CREATION

If you look at Figure 3, you'll see a dotted line between LISTEN and DECLARE. That is just to visually separate the activities that deepen connection from the activities that co-create on the earth. Kingdom prayer is designed to do both. Every prayer type or model you use so far is designed to connect you to the heart of the Father, the authority of Jesus, and the power of the Holy Spirit to release from Heaven what is needed for that situation. When the disciples wondered in awe why they could not cast out the demon, Jesus said, *"This kind can come out by nothing but prayer and fasting"* (Mark 9:29 NKJV). What kind of prayer and fasting? I do not know, but it is the kind of prayer and fasting where you connect to the heart of the Father, the authority of Jesus, and the power of the Holy Spirit to release from Heaven what is needed for that situation. The disciples had never come in contact with a demoniac like that before, so they were unsure of the approach necessary to handle a principality in the system of darkness. How do you know how to handle it? You learn through TALK ♦ ASK ♦ LISTEN™. All prayer, regardless of what *specialty*, is designed to bring the atmosphere of Heaven into Earth through connection with God.

Pray the Kingdom Way Prayer Prompt#2: *In this section, I talked about the Kingdom Prayer Framework. Ask God to bring to mind examples of when you engaged in the Kingdom Prayer Framework (TALK ♦ ASK ♦ LISTEN ♦ DECLARE ♦ DECREE™).*

CHAPTER 3

PRAYERS ANSWERED 100% OF THE TIME

When God told me to create the Pray The Kingdom Way Course, I said, *"Yes, on one condition."* I said, *"God, if I'm going to write a course on Kingdom Prayer, the number one question I'm going to get is, 'Why didn't God answer my prayer?' So if I create this, you have to answer that question for the people in a way that does NOT blame the people. None of this... 'You didn't pray enough'... 'Enough people weren't praying'... 'You must have some secret sin in your life'... 'My ways are higher than your way'... garbage."*

As you can tell, I was a little indignant. I didn't want to create a course on prayer anyway. For me, creating a course on prayer was like another Black person doing Diversity and Inclusion work. There are plenty that are called to do it. I ain't one of them. *Another* woman writing about prayer? Stormie Omartian and Priscilla Schirer had that on lock. No need for me to enter those streets. I was trying to grow my Executive Coaching business, and, at the time, I felt this prayer thing was a distraction from that. Because I didn't want to do it anyway, I figured there was no harm in being bold in this. My expectation was that He was going to give me some reason why prayers aren't answered, and I could say that such and such author wrote about that reason in their book on prayer and I'd be off the hook. In truth, I was so sick and tired of all the clichés tossed out to placate people who experienced the profound disappointment of not seeing the result they expected. In all fairness, there *were* times when I did have sin and a lack of faith in my life. But what about the other times, when faith was high and expectation was unwavering? I know it was those "unanswered prayers" that made people stumble and question God's love and goodness. I was a witness because it happened to me. I knew the answer was far deeper than just harboring secret sin. I said, *God, you have to answer this question.* And He did.

ANSWERED PRAYERS

What did God say when I asked how are You going to answer, "Why didn't God answer my prayer?" Ready for it? He said, *"Julia, I always answer prayer."* I wish I could insert a GIF of the slow blink and confused look I had on my face when I heard that. God always answers prayer. Every prayer Jesus prayed was answered—every single one. He is our example, and every prayer He prayed and still prays (remember He's always making intercession for us) was and is answered. The question itself is flawed. You may be thinking, *I want to believe you, Julia, but I can think of several prayers that He didn't answer.* I get it. I said the same thing when He said that. My cousin, Travis, was in a horrific accident when we were seventeen years old. He ended up on life support and his eldest sister, who was his guardian, had to decide whether to take him off life support or keep him on. While praying for my cousin, I heard God very clearly say that Travis was going to live, and I was to tell his sister that he would live. I was just a kid. His oldest sister was grown and responsible for his care since their parents passed. I was scared and nervous. I had never heard God like that and was terrified to say something. After days of mustering the courage, I told his sister what I heard. Afterwards, I never felt so full of faith the way I did. I was fully expecting a miracle. The decision was made to take him off life support. *"No problem,"* I thought, *"he's going to start breathing on his own and shock all the doctors."* The machine was turned off. His breaths slowed until they stopped. *"No problem, I thought, now it's miracle time baby! I can't wait."* Then came the sound of the flat line. I still wasn't deterred. *"Oh God, you're gonna do a resurrection?"* I rationalized. *"Sweet, this is gonna be so dope!"* And I held the expectation that resurrection was going to happen, and I was going to hear that he was resurrected in the mortuary when they were preparing him for burial. When that didn't happen, I attended his funeral waiting for life to quicken his mortal body in front of everyone. I imagined the move of God that would break out when people saw him come back to life and sit up in the casket. I was ready. When the services ended and he was loaded into the hearse and we began the drive to the burial site, I was excited because I just knew the resurrection was going to happen when we arrived at the burial site and as they were lowering the casket. He was going to burst through the coffin alive. I was ready. When the casket lowered without incident and the dirt was placed atop of him, I ran out of imagination. I didn't know how God was going to answer this prayer anymore, but I was still ready for Him to do it. Some would have called it denial, but I wasn't denying that he had died. I wasn't denying he was embalmed, had a funeral, or was buried in the ground. I held on to what God said, He was going to live. I was fully convinced that God was going to do a miracle. But He did not. I don't know when it hit, but the shock, anger, and embarrassment hit, and it hit hard. "But God, you said…" I cried in utter bewilderment. I shut God out for a long time after that incident with my cousin. I asked myself over and over what I did that I missed God. Why didn't I fast during that time? Why didn't I pray more? I reviewed the actions and the words I heard from God over and over. Did I take too long from the time He said to tell my family to do so? Was that disobedience? And did that void what He said? If God was always good and right, then the error was in me, I reasoned. I spent years asking God to search out the error because I was convinced that God didn't answer that prayer because of something I did… or didn't do. I was incredibly disappointed and shaken by the audacity of that request and the lack of an answer to that prayer. I pushed God aside and swept my feelings under the rug.

And that incident wasn't the last. There have been many incidents since where I stepped out on faith and did not meet the expected end. Some said it wasn't a faith issue but a belief issue. So I studied about belief in the Bible. Some said it wasn't a belief issue but a faith issue. So I studied about faith. Some said it had nothing to do with me because other people, with their own free will, were involved. Some said demonic activity was in the works. So I studied about demons and angels to understand better. No one ever had an answer that satisfied until God said, *"I always answer prayer. The question itself is flawed. The question presumes I don't answer. The real question needs to be first, how did I answer and second, what are we going to do when you don't like my answer?"*

If God always answers prayers, then the question becomes *How did He answer?* So when He said to create the course, from which this book was derived, I had decades of "unanswered prayer" incidents to reflect on. I began going back through the annals of my history looking for how God answered all those prayers. In the most simplest terms, His answer is either a yes or a no. But not just a yes or no. There is nuance. I came across an article entitled, *"Five Ways God Answers Prayer"*[7] that talked about the nuance in answers so powerfully. I had to include it, with some of my own explanations of course. God answers prayer in five ways:

1. No

God answers prayer with a No. No is an answer. You might not like it, but it's an answer. You might not understand why He said no, but it is an answer. I had a huge crush on the R&B singer Usher when I was a teen. *"God, can Usher be my boyfriend?" "No."* I looked back and thought, *"Good looking out on that one, God."* There are some situations where you got a NO from God and are so glad you did. That business deal. That client. That move. That relationship. That haircut. You can look back on

---
[7] (Palau 2004)

some of those NOs and see God's protection, provision, and love. And it makes you happy. It draws you closer to God. No is the right answer sometimes. We must be mature enough to understand that. When you understand that God is good and loving, even His NOs will be acts of His goodness and loving kindness towards you.

2. Yes, but you will have to wait.

"Wait for the Lord; be strong and take heart and wait for the Lord." (Psalm 27:14 NIV)

Some answers are a yes, but you will have to wait for their manifestation. Why do you have to wait? I do not know. ASK Him. I am not God. I do not know why you have to wait; He does. Maybe you must wait *because* there is some maturity needed before you can conquer that territory, advance the Kingdom in that arena, or expand the reach of your business. I don't know. ASK Him. We are being trained so that we have not only fruit but fruit that remains. There are some places we're going where, when we arrive on the scene, we need to be fortified enough to stand and stay there. Maybe there are parts of your character that need to be refined before He gives you what you are asking for so you do not destroy it or it destroys you. I don't know. ASK Him. At twelve, my oldest son asked me all the time, "Mommy, can I drive?" I always respond, "Sure, let me see your license." I never said no. As soon as he produces his permit or license, I will hand over the keys. The answer is yes, but there are some conditions you need to meet first. Maybe there are things, completely outside of your knowledge or control, that need to line up before it can happen. Remember when I said I had a hard time trusting God with my career? Back when I was making career decisions, the field I am in today wasn't formed or ready yet. Thirty years ago, being a Social Media Manager for a company wasn't a thing, so those called to it had to wait until the idea and technology were invented and infiltrated society before they could have a job.

3. Yes, but it won't be what you expect.

This was the answer from the Lord concerning my cousin's death. When I finally faced the issue and allowed God to talk to me about him, I asked, *"How did you answer this prayer?"* He said, "He is alive." My reply was, "Ummm, no, he is dead, and we buried him. There is a grave with his tombstone and everything." The Lord replied, "No, he is not dead. He is living with Me. I said Yes, but it was not as you expected." That answer deepened my relationship with God, and more answers poured out after I stopped being too mad to even talk to Him about it.

We see this a lot in business. "Lord, can I have a successful business?" "Yes, you can, but your successful business might not come in the product, service, or industry that you thought. The reason we must stay in partnership is so that I can direct you toward what is really best for you."

4. Yes, and here is more.

God is a God of excess. He is not skimpy. We ask, "God, may I have some peace in this situation?" His response is, "Yes, you can have peace, and I will give it to you in overflowing measure until it surpasses your understanding."

> *"God is able to do exceedingly above all that we can ask or think."* (Ephesians 3:20 NIV)

The Lord desires to lavish things upon us.

> *"I have come that you may have life and have it more abundantly."* (John 10:10 NKJV)

When I finally agreed to do the Pray The Kingdom Way course, I asked Him how I was going to fill it. He gave me a strategy. Pedro Adao was teaching on Challenges, and so we decided I would use that. I asked. "God, can I have 100 people in the prayer challenge?" "Yes! How about

200?" I had to upgrade my Zoom® account because people were telling my admin that they couldn't get in the Zoom room because we'd reached our current capacity.

5. Yes, I thought you would never ask!

When God told me directly that I did not love Him nor trust Him, I was astounded. I fought it tooth and nail before finally admitting it and completely pouring out my soul. I asked Him to take it from me, and He replied, "Thank you. Now we are finally getting somewhere. I am so glad you finally asked." This answer isn't about being literal. Of course, God knows you would ask. I love this answer because it shows the good, kind, and loving nature of God. He will wait patiently for His kids to realize, understand, or accept. There are some ways of thinking that He's just waiting for you to let Him into. As a Black woman, I was told that I had to work twice as hard, to only be considered half as good. There is some racism and sexism contributing to why I was taught that. Nonetheless, I was. Even though I hated that postulate, I never asked God about it. It wasn't until I was trying to do something and came up against crazy racism and sexism that in exasperation, I tossed out, "I don't want to work twice as hard." To which God was like, *"Great, can I take this from you?"* There is a scripture that talks about the sins of the father being visited on the sons (Numbers 14:18). I'd always heard this preached as if God would punish my kids if I didn't get my act together. I didn't like it, but I just accepted that viewpoint. That was until Dubb Alexander taught about it in School of Kingdom. The more accurate interpretation painted a good, kind, loving heavenly Father asking, *may I take that from you?* If the first generation says no, He'll ask the next and so on until someone in the line says *yes, take this.* What are those things that you are not ready to pour out in prayer? God has the overwhelming capacity to remove your burdens.

> *"Casting all your cares upon Him, for HE cares for you."*
> (1 Peter 5:7 ESV)

The moment you cast the burden you're carrying on God, His answer will always be, *"Yes, I am so glad you finally asked."*

"God, do You have an idea about what my business is and what I am supposed to do?"

"Yes, I am so glad you finally asked."

"What is my offer? Do You have an idea about what my offer is or the service that I am supposed to provide, the product that I am supposed to create?"

"Yes, I am so glad you finally asked."

Surprise! God always answers prayer. You may not like His answer, but He always answers.

> *"I thought, 'How I long to make you my sons, and give you a desirable land, the most beautiful inheritance to all the nations.' I thought, 'You would call me 'My Father' and never turn away from me."* (Jeremiah 3:19 CSB)

"How I long to make you my sons."

God has good things in store for us that He longs to give us if we would just ask.

> *"But while the son was still a long way off, his father saw him and was filled with compassion. He ran, threw his arms around his neck, and kissed him."* (Luke 15:20 CSB)

"Can I come home?"

"I am so glad you asked. Absolutely."

All of Heaven rejoices when a lost soul comes home. The heart of the Father is to see His family reunited and expanding. How people come into the Kingdom and what language they use to get there is of no concern to God. He answers willing hearts, not traditional fanfare.

So, what happens when you do not *see* the answers now that you know God always answers prayer? Ask Him how He answered it!

WHEN THE ANSWER HURTS!

Since God always answers prayer, what do we do when the answer hurts? Remember God the Father is, always has been and always will be loving and good. Therefore, every answer to prayer reflects His love and goodness--even when the answer hurts. Have you ever had a no that hurt? Or a yes that brought you pain? What do you do with those? The answer is you TALK ◆ ASK ◆ LISTEN™. The healing you seek for those are only found in God. The truth is I cannot tell you the reason He gave an answer that hurt. The answer is found in Him. I had some TALK ◆ ASK ◆ LISTEN™ about whether to offer reasons why God might say no. The only ones I am allowed to highlight is this: God won't go against His own Word, and He won't violate someone's free will. When Jesus was led into the wilderness to be tempted, He never let go of the Word or His position.

When you embrace that God always answers prayer, you will have a 100% answered prayer ratio. You will never question whether God answers *your* prayers. The reason the enemy wants to keep us guessing, even as people of God, as people of prayer, is because he desires our confidence and our agreement with what it is *he* wants to see manifest in the earth. If we do not approach God with confidence and agreement regardless of the answer, then we are not walking in trust. *Praying the Kingdom Way* shifts your focus from *if* to expecting and looking for the *how.* When you accept that God always answers prayer, you will have confidence to pray about *anything,* knowing that both the process of asking and the answer are a reflection of God's love and goodness toward you. When the scripture says, "Come boldly," you can because you know He always answers you.

Jesus said, *"Father, I know You always hear Me, but for the sake of these people... Lazarus come forth."* (John 11 42-43 ESV)

Jesus had confidence when He prayed about anything, including raising the dead. It bears repeating. When you pray the Kingdom way, you know that the process of asking, engaging, talking, listening, and seeing is our way of deeply committing to partnership, and it is for our good.

When you get that God always answers prayers, you will never wonder whether you *performed* enough to see your prayers answered. When you take the Kingdom Prayer Framework approach to prayer, you are co-creating with God. You are coming from a place of relationship, not performance.

EXPECTATION

Expectation is more about trust in the Answerer than *your* need or dependence on the answer. Did you catch that? We have, especially in American Western society, an extremely high results-oriented culture, and it seeps into the church, and that includes prayer. We put more emphasis on the outcome than we do our trust in the One who answers prayer.

> *"And when he came to the house, the blind men came to Him. Jesus said, 'Do you believe that I am able to do this?' They said to Him, 'Yes, Lord.' Then He touched their eyes saying, 'According to your faith let it be to you.'"* (Matthew 9:28-29 NKJV)

Jesus will always ask you, *"Do you believe that I am able to do this?"* Because it was not about the outcome of the man's eyes being opened, it was about trust and belief.

> *"Suddenly, a man with leprosy approached him and knelt before him. 'Lord,' the man said, 'If you are willing, you can heal me and make me clean.' Jesus reached out and touched him. 'I am willing,'*

he said. 'Be healed!' And instantly the leprosy disappeared." (Matthew 8:2-3 NLT)

Trust is key. *"Lord, if You are willing."* I trust that You can if You are willing. Jesus said, *"Yes, I am willing."*

A lot of us were instructed to go to God with the "If You can do anything, please do something" mentality. Based on what you've learned thus far, the *if this be your will* is not the end of the prayer but the beginning. Traditional prayer weakens faith while Kingdom prayer strengthens it.

"Well, I have no say in this, so I'm going to toss it up to You to see if You feel like doing it. You're an indifferent and mean God, so who knows; maybe if I bug You enough, then You will answer me because I was persistent." That is not how it is meant to be in the Kingdom.

When we read the parable in Luke 18: 1-8, the story of the unjust judge, too often we associate the unjust judge in that parable to be God and the beggar to be us. Too often in prayer, we do things and say things in hopes that our persistence will cause God to change His mind and answer our requests. The truth that is being revealed is similar to the truth revealed in Matthew 7:11 when Jesus said, *"...If you, then, though you are evil, know how to give good gifts to your children, how much more will your Father in heaven give good gifts to those who ask him!"* The point is that if we are capable of giving and doing good to those we love just because they ask, how much more is God able and willing to do for us. God is just, and we are not beggars. We are royal children. We don't persist because we're trying to change God's mind. We persist in Kingdom prayer because we're climate changers and atmosphere adjusters with the full backing of Heaven.

SIGHT

In partnership with God through prayer you can expect to see evidence for that which you prayed. It begs the question, what are you looking for?

> *"And the Lord said to Abram after Lot had separated from him: 'Lift your eyes now and look from the place where you are—northward, southward, eastward, and westward, for all the land which you see I give to you to your descendants forever.'"* (Genesis 13:14-15 NKJV)

"Lift up your eyes and look from the place where you are." He had to instruct Abram to look in all directions: north, south, east, and west. Look in all directions, for what? For the promise. *"You will see the land that I will give to you and your descendants forever."* What are you looking for?

> *"And he said to his servant, 'Go up now, look toward the sea.' So he went up and looked, and said, 'There is nothing.' And seven times he said, 'Go again.'"* (1 Kings 18:43 NKJV)

What are you looking for, and how many times are you willing to look?

> *"Moreover, the word of the Lord came to me, saying, 'Jeremiah, what do you see?' And I said, 'I see a branch of an almond tree.'"* (Jeremiah 1:11 NKJV)

> *"And the word of the Lord came to me the second time, saying, 'What do you see?' And I said, 'I see a boiling pot, and it is facing away from the north.'"* (Jeremiah 1:13 NKJV)

> *"Then the Lord said to me, 'What do you see, Jeremiah?' And I said, 'Figs, the good figs, very good; and the bad, very bad, which cannot be eaten, they are so bad.'"* (Jeremiah 24:3 NKJV)

> *"I will stand my watch and set myself on the rampart and watch to see what He will say to me, and what I will answer when I am corrected."* (Habakkuk 2:1 NKJV)

> *"Ask, and it will be given to you; seek, and you will find; knock, and it will be opened to you."* (Matthew 7:7 NKJV)

The evidence of God's goodness and the evidence of God answering prayer is clearer than we have trained our eyes to see. "Seek and you will find." If you are looking for evidence about why God will not answer your prayer, and why He seems indifferent, with the help of the enemy, that is exactly what you will find. So many have more confidence in God's ability than in His willingness. When we hold doubt, we will look for evidence that supports doubt. We will see evidence contrary to what is actually happening, just because it is what we seek. My expectation is not in the answer that I want; my expectation is in the One who can back up what He said. I am expecting an answer to show up because He always answers prayer. When I craft prayer with the One who created prayer, my faith is limitless. What would change for you if you simply believe that God always answered prayer? What will you pray for knowing that all your prayers are answered? What does that say about God?

Pray the Kingdom Way Prayer Prompt #3: *Show me an example of a prayer You answered but I didn't either recognize or like the answer You gave.*

PART II

INTRODUCTION PART II:

FOR THE KINGDOM MINDED FOUNDER, CEO OR LEADER IN BUSINESS

As I mentioned in the preface, this book is divided into two parts. Part 1 was designed to present and make the case for the Kingdom Prayer Framework. That part can be used by anyone who wants to experience more freedom and power in prayer regardless of your mountain of influence. This part of the book is specifically for my Kingdom entrepreneurs, founders, and business leaders. For those of you who know that your lane is business and want to understand how to use your business and business dealing to expand the Kingdom of God, this one's for you. For those of you who aren't in business but are curious about these matters, welcome! This section is about helping you shift the way you view business and money. In Chapters 4, 5, and 6, I will stretch your thinking and introduce some ideas. In Chapter 7, I will put all the ideas together with case studies from real businesses.

Before we begin, engage in TALK ♦ ASK ♦ LISTEN™ about how to receive what you are about to read. It will challenge your thinking. I am not here to convince you of anything but to introduce you to some ideas that have the potential to change your life if you let them. In this section, I am going to get even more mystical and talk about visions, angels, and even the conversations I have had with inanimate objects. If these offend your sensibilities, stop reading, and go TALK to God about why you're offended. But if you are my people, then these things will not offend your sensibilities at all. In fact, this section will probably confirm or affirm some of the "strange" encounters or thoughts you've had. Again, even if you agree with me, go TALK to God. I am catalytic, and what I convey tends to be the spark for many. The beauty of a book is that you can put it down if the Holy Spirit arrests you. Let Him. If He *interrupts* your reading to TALK to you or ASK you questions, stop reading and engage. That's the point. Record the encounters and go after their interpretation. How you interpret the encounters is more important than having them. You will never get the correct interpretation without the wisdom of God, so go TALK to the One who created wisdom.

CHAPTER 4

THE PURPOSE OF BUSINESS IN THE KINGDOM

Business Is Not Church

I've always wanted to honor God in my business but had no clue what that looked like. Like most, I decided to replicate what I saw in church in business as much as possible. There are many movements and moves about how to do so. The marketplace ministry focus was great because it validated that business was on God's mind. It fell short because it reduced business into being a territory for Kingdom expansion instead of a vehicle of Kingdom expansion. What do I mean? A lot of the marketplace ministry movement focused on your job or business as a mission field and thereby tried to turn everyone into workplace evangelists who felt pressure to proselytize their workplace with gospel, even if it was illegal to do so in some places. I attended classes where people had lawyers tell you the law and how to handle it when opposed at work. People began taking a "stand" for God and refused to do their job or defied company policy for the sake of the "gospel". Under that approach, business was viewed as just another evil-filled place that needed the gospel of Jesus and more angry, defiant Christians taking a stand for their faith.

I'm not saying that you should never talk to someone about Jesus in a work situation. Nor am I saying that there aren't instances when God tells someone to take a stand on the legality of a practice. But we've treated business like that's all it's good for—a toy that we're playing tug of war with Satan to see who gets to have it. What if that's incomplete? Without the revelation that business was God's idea, and that God has a reason and purpose for it, we treat business like a thing to conquer rather than a vehicle for conquering. We try to make it look as much like our religious traditions as possible with more Bible studies at work. We pray for the Spirit to "fall" like we see on Sunday mornings in charismatic churches, not realizing that, if everyone was "slain" in the spirit, that would be a terribly unproductive day with so many potential OSHA violations. I was TALKing to God about this one day, and He said, *"You're disrespecting your business."* Shocked, I asked what He meant. He said, *"You keep trying to treat and turn your business into a church when it is not."* This sparked a long discussion. If you've ever heard of Lance Wallnau's seven mountains strategy, you can get this. In brief, he posits that there are seven mountains that influence culture (business, education, church, entertainment, media, government and family), and those at the tops of those mountains get to control the influence. What I love about the seven mountain message is that, again, it showed that God cared about other industries and how our interests in these places were places for Kingdom expansion. Remember: *You shall be witnesses to me bringing wholeness (Jerusalem) to a place that delights you (Judea) as its careful guardian (Samaria)* (Acts 1:8). Unfortunately, the seven mountain message has been reduced to a fight to be the best, get to the, top, or argue about why or why not ascending to the top is "right." The problem is that if you get to have major influence in that industry, whether you are at the top or not, but you are influencing it without considering God's reason and purpose for those mountains, then whose agenda are you going to advocate?

In a vision, God showed me a skyscraper in a business district. On the top of the building was a giant phone receiver. You know, like the old-fashioned telephone that had a dial tone when you picked it up. It was resting on the top of the building. Then I saw contorted figures on the ground scramble to the building and start climbing the building.

Without words, God told me the goal of those creatures was to knock off the phone receiver so there was no open communication between God and the business and thus the industry.

The phone receiver was already at the top of the building. The threat was to knock it off. So many have been conditioned to believe that we must get to the tops of our industries because we must put the receiver there. The truth of the matter is, since God created that industry, the receiver has always been there. There is a new awakening among business owners to their responsibility to recognize that the receiver is already there, and then to amplify the communication. That is what Pray the Kingdom Way is about. It is about recognizing that the connection is already set.

The gospel of salvation is for humanity. The gospel of the Kingdom is for the redemption of the systems and creation. Business is not church. I had a client who struggled with this idea. He was in business and gave a lot of stuff away. His giving was causing major problems in his business. As his advisor, I asked him to consider not giving. He clutched his proverbial pearls. "Giving was essential to Christian life", he protested. But the scripture says in Proverbs 11:26 that people rejoice when grain is SOLD. The underlying issues had to deal with his view of money, which we'll talk more about in the next chapter, and his view of his business. Of course, giving isn't bad. But his actions violated the reason and purpose of business, which is why he was struggling so much. In my advisory work with leaders, there is usually an unconscious war happening inside the owner about the business. Instead of viewing the business world as a place to endure until Jesus returns, or a hostile environment that needs light to dispel the darkness, we as Kingdom believers need to view it differently. We need to view business as a vehicle for Kingdom expansion, no matter what the business is. It is easy to see business as a vehicle when your business sells tracks, Bibles, Jesus bumper stickers, or mints with scripture on them. But what about other businesses that aren't overtly Christian? Yes, those too are used for expansion. It is within the dominion of the God in connection with the business owner to explore and express how.

> *Then the seventh angel sounded: And there were loud voices in heaven, saying, "The Kingdoms of this world have become the Kingdoms of our Lord and of His Christ, and He shall reign forever and ever!* (Revelation 11:15 NKJV)

GOD'S REASON AND PURPOSE FOR BUSINESS

What is the reason and purpose of business in the Kingdom? If the Kingdom is God's extension of His governing system through us on the earth, then what is the role of business? To answer this, you have to understand that your business and profession was not your idea. Your business was God's idea. He then created you with everything that you would need to fulfill the function of the business that He placed inside of you.

The Reason for Business

> *"And Jabez called on the God of Israel saying, 'Oh, that You would bless me indeed, and enlarge my territory.'"* (1 Chronicles 4:10 NKJV)

What was God's plan? To establish a family, establish a government, and expand them both. **The reason business exists is for greater reach.** Reason reflects what's in God's heart. God is always creating ways to reach more people.

> *"I will certainly bless you. I will multiply your descendants beyond number, like the stars in the sky and the sand on the seashore. Your descendants will conquer the cities of their enemies. And through your descendants all the nations of the earth will be blessed—all because you have obeyed me."* (Genesis 22:17-18 NLT)

I could invite 200 people to come to church, but most of them won't come. However, I can get 200 people to buy a product or attend a class that I created, and they'd show up. The reach of the Kingdom is exponentially multiplied through business. I am a reflection of God, and He dwells inside of me. I am made in His image to do exactly what He is doing in Heaven. Because of that, I can reach people through business that I may never be able to reach through a traditional ministry. And your business does not have to be overtly Christian or a ministry look-a-like for it to reach people. If you want to put scripture on your restaurant's drink cups, you can. But you can also have a massage business that allows people to feel the peace and relaxation they need.

One of my clients loved horses and was very much into the rodeo scene. But as a woman, she saw some problems that other women in that industry faced, too. She created something specifically for people in rodeo because through her being in rodeo, God could reach more people.

All the disciples were marketplace people. They were all businesspeople. They had a place in a profession that gave them a platform. Why did God call the disciples? Because their profession allowed them to have more reach, and their professions taught them how to reach people. He literally said, "Follow Me and I will make you fishers of men" (Matthew 4:19), because that is reach. Not only are they going out to fish, trade and connect with other trade ports, but they are also selling the fish to different groups of people that they may not ever have had the opportunity to encounter otherwise. Reach is a concentric circle. It begins where you are and then expands outward. You can go to greater places through business.

THE PURPOSE OF BUSINESS

So it was, as the multitude pressed about Him to hear the word of God, that He stood by the Lake of Gennesaret, and saw two boats standing by the lake; but the fishermen had gone from them and

> *were washing their nets. Then He got into one of the boats, which was Simon's, and asked him to put out a little from the land. And He sat down and taught the multitudes from the boat.*
>
> *When He had stopped speaking, He said to Simon, "Launch out into the deep and let down your nets for a catch."*
>
> *But Simon answered and said to Him, "Master, we have toiled all night and caught nothing; nevertheless at Your word I will let down the net." And when they had done this, they caught a great number of fish, and their net was breaking. So they signaled to their partners in the other boat to come and help them. And they came and filled both the boats, so that they began to sink.* (Luke 5:1-7 NKJV)

You've probably read or heard this passage with a "launch into the deep" or a "nevertheless at Your word" emphasis. However, this is an unrecognized example of wealth creation and distribution. Why do I say that? Because after they had that haul, Jesus said, *"Do not be afraid, from now on you will catch men"* (Luke 5:10 NKJV). Peter had a family, and he was not expected to forsake his family and leave his profession as a fisherman to follow Jesus for three years. The haul that day was so great that the wealth created from it allowed those fishermen to take a sabbatical from their fishing professions to go train with Jesus for three years and not be in deficit. The haul from that load blessed the other people in the industry. It blessed their competitors; it created wealth for them. It took care of the people because the haul from that load had to be disseminated to people; it had to be sold.

> *"Blessed shall you be in the city, and blessed shall you be in the country. Blessed shall be the fruit of your body, the produce of your ground and the increase of your herds, the increase of your cattle and the offspring of your flocks. Blessed shall be your basket and your kneading bowl. Blessed shall you be*

when you come in, and blessed shall you be when you go out." (Deuteronomy 28:3-6 NKJV)

People in the city and the people in the field during the time of Jesus were blessed because there was an overabundance of fish. Industries were literally birthed from this haul and the business strategy that had been given to them by God. The net makers received an upgrade in their business as a result of what took place with this particular haul. Those who preserved food received an upgrade because of what took place with that haul. Business strategies had to change in order to protect that harvest.

The purpose of business is to create wealth, opportunity, connections, and ideas to take care of people. The purpose of business is not just to create enough for you; it is to partner with wealth to take care of a multitude of people.

> *"Go therefore and make disciples of all the nations."* (Matthew 28:19; Mark 16:15)

Do you believe that Chick-fil-A™ is discipling people through their chicken nuggets and their chicken sandwiches? Yes, they are. They have established a way of doing that because there is a governing system over Chick-fil-A™. When you say thank you to someone at Chick-fil-A™, their governing system dictates that that employee responds with, "My pleasure."

> *2 Corinthians 9:8 states, "And God is able to make all grace," meaning empowerment, "abound to you, so that in all things, at all times having all you need, you will abound in every good work."* (NKJV)

The purpose of business is to create wealth to take care of people. All things, at all times, and all that you need will abound to you in every good work. Your business is a good work; business in the Kingdom is a good work.

The reason business exists is for greater reach.

The purpose for which it exists is to create wealth, opportunity, connections, and ideas to take care of people.

CREATION THROUGH THE LENS OF BUSINESS

Let's take a look at the creation story through the lens of business.

> *In the beginning God created the heavens and the earth. The earth was formless and empty, and darkness covered the deep waters. And the Spirit of God was hovering over the surface of the waters.*
>
> *Then God said, "Let there be light," and there was light. And God saw that the light was good. Then he separated the light from the darkness. God called the light "day" and the darkness "night."*
>
> *And evening passed and morning came, marking the first day.*
>
> *Then God said, "Let there be a space between the waters, to separate the waters of the heavens from the waters of the earth." And that is what happened. God made this space to separate the waters of the earth from the waters of the heavens. God called the space "sky."*
>
> *And evening passed and morning came, marking the second day.*
>
> *Then God said, "Let the waters beneath the sky flow together into one place, so dry ground may appear." And that is what happened. God called the dry ground "land" and the waters "seas." And God saw that it was good. Then God said, "Let the land sprout with vegetation—every sort of seed-bearing plant, and trees that grow seed-bearing fruit. These seeds will then produce the kinds of plants and trees from which they came." And that is what happened. The*

land produced vegetation—all sorts of seed-bearing plants, and trees with seed-bearing fruit. Their seeds produced plants and trees of the same kind. And God saw that it was good.

And evening passed and morning came, marking the third day. (Genesis 1:1-13 NLT)

What was the previous state? The earth was formless and empty. God had an idea and brought forth light. As entrepreneurs, God gives us ideas because there is a problem that requires a solution or because an innovation demands something new comes forth. We typically tie the solutions to those problems to some business.

When God separated the land, the sky, and the water, He was giving organizational structure to His creation. What is the organizational structure for your business? There must be structure because we need to know who does what and when, how we are supposed to operate, and what our legal entity is.

Then God said, "Let lights appear in the sky to separate the day from the night. Let them be signs to mark the seasons, days, and years. Let these lights in the sky shine down on the earth." And that is what happened. God made two great lights—the larger one to govern the day, and the smaller one to govern the night. He also made the stars. God set these lights in the sky to light the earth, to govern the day and night, and to separate the light from the darkness. And God saw that it was good.

And evening passed and morning came, marking the fourth day.

Then God said, "Let the waters swarm with fish and other life. Let the skies be filled with birds of every kind." So God created great sea creatures and every living thing that scurries and swarms in the water, and every sort of bird—each producing offspring of the same kind. And God saw that it was good. Then God blessed

> *them, saying, "Be fruitful and multiply. Let the fish fill the seas, and let the birds multiply on the earth."*
>
> *And evening passed and morning came, marking the fifth day.*
>
> *Then God said, "Let the earth produce every sort of animal, each producing offspring of the same kind—livestock, small animals that scurry along the ground, and wild animals." And that is what happened. God made all sorts of wild animals, livestock, and small animals, each able to produce offspring of the same kind. And God saw that it was good.* (Genesis 1:14-25 NKJV)

In this passage, we see an idea, we see purpose, we see organizational structure, and then He gives a *vision*. There must be a vision to see where you are going with a priority establishment. What is the priority of the business right now? We must set KPIs, key performance indicators. Once that is established, He institutes product development. Every product—fish, vegetation, animals, birds—that God added to the earth was for product development. He made sure that every product He placed into His "business" could reproduce. Our businesses must be able to reproduce in order to get more clients and continue to grow.

The model for the Kingdom is that there is a ruler, there is a way, and there is a place. The model that creation shows us is that there is an idea, there is purpose, there is a structure, there is the vision, there is the priority establishment, and there is a product.

The role of business in the Kingdom is to be the extension of God's governing system to generate and distribute wealth, opportunity, connections, and ideas to take care of and benefit all people. The Kingdom works everywhere. Therefore, people who do not know God can apply the Kingdom principles and see it work because the Kingdom is for the benefit of all. Again, God wanted to establish a family, establish a government, and expand them both.

YOUR BUSINESS IS A COLONY OF HEAVEN

If you have a business, you have core values, and this is likened to your way of ruling; this is your governing system. These are principles that undergird how you run your business, also part of your governing system. Your *place* to rule is your target market. Your target market might be your region or specific people in a demographic, psychographic, or a specific location.

The product or services that you provide is your hook, the way that you reach out to people with your product or service. People buy your products and services; you grow the business; you hire more people, or your business has vendors with whom you can partner. Then you can partner with greater systems. The bigger your business gets, the more publicity it gets; the greater the influence you have, the more people you can reach. Marketing in business is all about letting people know what you do so they can come and find you, so they can partake of what it is that you do.

You as the business owner are the ruler. You have a USP, a unique sales proposition, which makes you stand out from others. As the business owner, *you* reflect God. *You* are a combination of your skills, gifts, personality, quirks, and passion. *You* are going to influence the way your business is governed, and it is going to set you apart. Your business has a specific product or service that God wants to use to extend His reach to the world.

Wealth does not always mean money; wealth can also be people. Part of what God wants to do in and through you as business owners and as employers is to heal His people from oppressive leadership. Say someone has had a bad boss in their lifetime—and we have all had a bad boss in our lifetime— and they come in as an employee of *your* company. Because you are charged with extending God's governing system and God wants to establish a family, you get to interact with these employees differently. You have the opportunity to treat them in a manner that is different from what they have been used to.

Because you are extending reach, you are showing what is different about your business based on the heart you have for what God has called you to do. Through you, all people benefit, not just the people who buy your product or services, but the people who work for you and those that contract with you. Through you, all people are to be blessed to generate and distribute wealth.

When you get this, and when you understand the role of business, when you understand that God's Kingdom is an extension of His way of doing things in the earth that reflects Heaven through you, then you will stop thinking of yourself as some sort of second-class citizen who is "only doing this" until you can get into "real ministry."

When you capture this new Kingdom identity for your business, you then understand that you are free from thinking that making money, and lots of it, is an unholy goal. Because your business was God's idea, you must go to God about what He wants to do with it. Again, the resources and provisions available are the responsibility of the One who created it. That is why you need to know that your business was not your idea so that you can stop putting the pressure on yourself to sustain it. It was God's idea; therefore, it is His responsibility to sustain it. According to His reasoning and according to His purpose for your business, God has the provisions necessary for that sustenance already earmarked for you in Heaven.

If God has called you to reach people in rural America, then the provisions will look different than if God called you to reach people in Beverly Hills. The provisions needed in a large city will not be the same as what's needed in the bush. Do not compare your business to someone else's. Because assignments are different, comparison is foolish. I can compare mine to what God has said my business is supposed to do.

When I connect with God about my financial projections, He can tell me, "You are over," or "You are under," or "We need to do this or that so we can continue to move forward." Then I do not have to feel slimy about making money, about coming up with new products or services because my product or service reproduced. God established my business that way.

Your products and services carry within them a reproductive factor.

That is why I believe in the parable of the talent when the servant hid his money and the master said, *"So you ought to have deposited my money with the bankers, and at my coming I would have received back my own with interest"* (Matthew 25:27 NKJV). The talent had within it the ability to reproduce itself, and that the person who was in charge, the ruler of that product, suppressed that product from reproducing after its kind. It was a mismanagement of the servant's responsibility. The way we as business owners suppress our products, suppress what God wants to do, is by having faulty beliefs about business, about money, about our customers, and about who we are. God wants to free your thinking, for you to see your business as a personalized reflection of God's love for you.

If I have this idea that God only wants to use me for His benefit, but He does not really care about me, then I am going to withhold myself from seeking Him and what He really wants to do because I am going to be afraid of His answer!

The moment you catch the revelation that God created the thing that you were to rule over in a way that reflects, enhances, and requires all the best parts of your personality, your preferences, and your makeup, then you see your business as a personalized reflection of God's love for you. You will then begin to pray for your business with confidence knowing that your business is an extension of God's goodness and love *to you* and to your customers. The enemy will no longer trick you into thinking you are not serving God by being in business.

Pray the Kingdom Way Prayer Prompt #4: *Ask, if I accepted that business was about expanding reach to create wealth, opportunity, connections, and ideas to take care of people, then what is my business's part in your plan?*

CHAPTER 5

YOUR BUSINESS'S IDENTITY IN HEAVEN

Don't start with why. Start with who. But the who I'm referring to is not your customer. Simon Sinek's book <u>Start With Why</u> is an amazing book. It gives great insight on how organizations can communicate the why of their brand to inspire brand loyalty to both internal and external customers. However, I respectfully disagree with starting with why, especially if you are a Christian in business. In the Kingdom, God doesn't begin with why. He begins with who. Everything that was and is came from the Who of God through Jesus. Whenever God is inspiring change on Earth, He begins with identity.

At the baptism of Jesus in Matthew 3:17, Mark 1:11, and Luke 3:22, the scripture records the Holy Spirit descending on Jesus in bodily form, and the Heavens declaring *who* He was.

> *"And a voice from heaven said, 'This is my Son, whom I love; with him I am well pleased.'"*

Though Jesus's baptism is mentioned in John, its recount does not mention this declaration from Heaven. I believe that is because of John's unique opening. Instead of focusing on the earthly and human genealogy of Jesus and His earthly predecessors, John takes us out of time and space and catapults us into Third Heaven reality to show us Jesus's identity. He opens with:

"In the beginning was the Word, and the Word was with God, and the Word was God." (John 1:1)

In the gospels, Jesus's announcement before he began public ministry was marked by a declaration of *who* He was. Being announced as the Son of God was scandalous in those times. It offended a lot of the religious people of the day. *How dare this man Jesus proclaim himself to be the son of God?* It was blasphemy to claim such closeness to God. Jesus came to remind the world of the closeness that all of humanity can have with God. Because, as you recall from our foundations, God's whole agenda on Earth is to establish a family, establish a kingdom, and expand them both. Jesus's public introduction to the world displays God's intent. From the Heavens, it was announced which facet of Jesus' identity would shape His work on Earth as Messiah and King. He was operating from the seat of Son. In Matthew, Mark, and Luke's accounts, we clearly see Jesus's public introduction to the world as God's son. From John's account, we clearly see Jesus's reincarnation from a spiritual being to a physical one. John's account shows us Jesus's authority in Heaven and on Earth, all because facets of His identity were proclaimed.

On a personal level, we understand according to Jeremiah 1:5 that each person on Earth was known by God before ever arriving on Earth. The gospel of salvation is all about reuniting us to the family we all came from in Heaven here on Earth. The gospel of the Kingdom is about unleashing the family and government of God to shape Earth into what our homeland looks like.

In your studies of the scriptures, you already know that names are important. Names give the shortest glimpse into a person's identity. The identity of a person is actually greater than their name, but a name highlights a facet of that identity. In the Bible, there are many accounts of giving a name, changing a name, or calling one by a name. Understanding names means understanding identity. In both the old and new testament,

God began every new assignment by revealing a new identity. The "who" reveals the "do." Not the other way around.

In my executive coaching work, I talk to my clients about their personal identity and how it is affecting them as leaders. A common topic I cover is how they have three identities. There is the *Internal Identity*. This is how you see yourself. It is an identity placed on you by you. We saw evidence of incorrect internal identity in Numbers 13:33 when the scouts came back and said, *"we are as grasshoppers in their sight."* Internal identity issues show in imposter syndrome and even in gender identity. Internal identity is linked to eating disorders, addiction, depression and anxiety. Then there is *External Identity*. This is how the world sees you. This is an identity placed on you by others. Being a "Karen" is an external identity. Being a "thug" is an external identity. Being "too much" is an external identity. Your reputation is an external identity. In my early days of business, I gravitated to Sally Hogshead's work with her book <u>Fascinate: How To Make Your Brand Impossible To Resist</u> because unlike the other personality tests that show you *how you see the world*, her work focused on *how the world sees you*. Her premise was simple, you are already perceived as fascinating so just lean into why they already like you. But this was all about external identity. We all have an image of who we want to be and how we want to be perceived. Growing up I wanted my external identity to be like Clair Huxtable from The Cosby Show. She exuded femininity, class, fun, and romance as a powerful and educated married Black woman with kids. People will steal, kill, and destroy if their internal and /or external identity is threatened. People will argue with themselves and others if their internal and/or external identity is threatened. Lastly, there is *Eternal Identity*. This is how Heaven sees you. This is the identity given to you by God Himself. It never changes, and He doesn't take it back. It is as expansive as the Heavens to accommodate everything you are called to do on the Earth at every stage you are called to do it. Newborns have a full and powerful eternal identity, but their assignment in the first months of life is not leading a global conglomerate. It's neck control.

Your eternal identity is as unique as your fingerprint. It is your unique marker in the world, and your places of influence recognize it in you. This is how all of the spiritual world and spiritual things interact with you. When the voice announced Jesus as Son, it announced part of His eternal identity. When the angel greeted Gideon, it greeted him with his eternal identity. When the angel greeted the mother Mary, it greeted her with her eternal identity.

Of all the identities, which one do you think is most important? Of all the identities you have, your *eternal* identity is the most important because it is the one that is the real you. Internal and external identities are useful, but they need to be submitted to the lordship of Christ in whom you were created. This is why people who reject God spend their lives defining and redefining themselves by their internal and external identities and demanding that others define them according to the definitions they set for themselves. In truth, you have to align your internal identity to your eternal one and see yourself as Christ sees you. We love to quote Psalm 139:14. *I praise you because I am fearfully and wonderfully made; your works are wonderful,* ***I know that full well.*** But not too much emphasis is on the last part. Do you know and are you fully convinced that you are a wonderful work? Isn't it about time we "know full well" the wonderful that is us. True humility is submitting to whatever God says. Submit to the idea that He thought enough of you to make you just like Him, give you an inheritance, a territory to rule, natural gifts, skills, and talents and then moved in on the inside of you so you'd never be alone. But wait, there's more! On top of that, He then set up a system of constant communication so you co-create and conquer with Him. So Ma'am or Sir, why are you wondering if this business thing is for you?

You have to align your external identity, which includes your behavior, reputation, and brand, to your eternal identity. This also means we have to be careful how we label and judge others. Internal and external identities are important, but they do not define you. Your eternal identity alone accomplished that job. Because of how God set things up on earth, the spirit realm recognizes your eternal identity, and it also recognizes if your internal or external identities are stronger to you than your eternal one. This is misalignment. It is the reason the sons of Sceva got smacked around by demons. They were trying to leverage internal and external identity to do supernatural work. One of my favorite Einstein quotes says, "we cannot solve our problems with the same thinking we used when we created them." This is why Jesus talked about renewing our minds, about faith, about the kingdom of heaven, etc. He was aligning us to Heaven's perspective. That's what ambassadors do. He gave us a guide for how to align our internal and external identities to our eternal, thus elevating the eternal above all.

If identity is important to a person, it is also important to a business. This is why I say start with who, the eternal who, not why. Countries, nations, cities, governments and companies all have an eternal identity in Heaven. On Earth, corporate identity is the external identity of the organization. Corporate culture is the internal identity of the organization. A lot of the branding, marketing, and PR is about crafting, projecting, and fixing external identity. Organizational and leadership development is about crafting, projecting, and fixing internal identity. I am convinced that a business (nation, city, or government too for that matter) will never achieve its highest and best until someone in that organization leans into the identity heaven gave that business. As business owners and leaders, especially if you are a founder, it is imperative that you know your business's identity in heaven.

Business identity is about understanding the reason and purpose God intended for *your* business, specifically, not just business in general. If the business mountain is about reach, and the purpose of the business mountain is to create wealth, opportunity, connections, and ideas to take care of people, you as the business owner, founder or one responsible for future casting must ask God, " what is Your reason and purpose for *my* business?"

When I was in high school, I had a crush on this boy. Everyone called him Okoye. I had many unrequited interests in high school, so I was delightfully shocked when he asked for my phone number and asked if he could call me sometime. I still wasn't allowed to have boys call my house, so I asked for his phone number instead. One day, I called him. I put on my best voice because I had "good home training," as the old folks would say. As I expected, an adult answered the phone. I cleared my throat and, as politely as I could said, "Good evening sir. My name is Julia. May I speak to Okoye please?" I expected the rustling sound the phone made when someone either covered the receiver with their hand or put it down on a hard surface as they leaned away to yell for that person to come to the phone. That didn't happen. Instead I got the most perplexing question from the other end of the line. The man asked, "Which one?"

"Which one?" I repeated. "Yes, which one? Five Okoyes live here." I had lost all eloquence as I stumbled through trying to describe as best I could the one I was looking for just for the man to tell me he wasn't home. What happened? I didn't realize that Okoye was the boy's last name! I didn't know his first name. Insert face palm emoji--or more appropriate for the time period, the pager code that when turned upside down, spelled LOSER. I had called the house without knowing how to identify the person I was looking for and stumbled my way around.

This story remained a memory of teenage embarrassment until I heard Dan McCollam teach on the importance of understanding your "first name" in the prophetic. The prophetic is so important in business, but I digress. Dano's teaching was very simple. When we come into the family of God, all the rights and privileges of being a part of that family (last name) are ours. Prophetic words given to an individual carry clues about that person's "first name" or their eternal identity. Likewise, the prophetic words about business carry clues about a business's eternal identity. Let me ask you, how can you do kingdom business without knowing the identity of your business? For most, the answer is, you guess. It becomes hit or miss. The eternal identity of the business doesn't change. You may stumble or even be led to an idea, product, service, or method that takes off like gangbusters because it accidentally aligned with the business's identity.

When I started my business in 2012, it was called Brave Communication. I had just gone out on my own after working for my mentor, Lynne Ruhl at Perfect 10 Corporate Cultures. I'd moved out of state, and with her blessing, I decided to do what we did at P-10 in Brave. I set up shop as a communications skills training company. I would go into workplaces and train leadership teams on soft-skill communication like listening, building trust, and valuing differences. When I looked at my track record in business and at work, I always had favor with the leaders. I got certified in executive and business coaching because I was drawn to leaders. Fast forward many years, and God told me to change the business name to Brave Leadership Consulting. While the business always focused on leaders, under its first name the focus was on communication. Under its current name, the focus is on leader development. I believe God was guiding me to align to Brave's eternal identity before I even had a grid for understanding what it was.

Brave Leadership Consulting is not me, and I am not her. She is an entity all her own with a tax id number and legal structure to prove it. Once I really understood the kingdom's eternal identity for myself and for my business, everything changed. I could see how they were linked. Remember, we were all in God before we got here; so Brave knew me and she knew me as her executive before there was a beginning. Because I saw her as an entity all her own created in Jesus, I engaged in conversation with Jesus about the business. Eventually Holy Spirit taught me to engage the business in conversation. I asked the business to talk to me, to tell me about herself. I began to ask my business about the relationships it wanted to build. We had a spiritual conversation that allowed me to get to know her in a deeper way. Part of my personal Identity Statement says, *I am Kingdom Authority. I am a fire-wielding, territory-taking releaser of pure promise who rules and reigns in my assignment with swift obedience and pungent wisdom, partnering with the heavenly realm to dismantle obstacles obstructing success.*

This identity statement shakes me to my core every time I read or recite it because of its accuracy. After I had this personal experience, Holy Spirit whispered that Brave has an identity statement too. I engaged in many cycles of TALK ♦ ASK ♦ LISTEN™ about the identity of my business, and listened to what He had to say about Brave. I listened for statements and then refined them until those statements spoke to me and we crafted Brave's Identity statement. Allow me to introduce you to my business as she is known and interacted with in the heavenlies. Brave, say hello to the people and introduce yourself.

> *I Am The Leadership Etiquette Of Heaven*
> *I Am An Encounter Of Wisdom*
> *I Am A Revealer Of Identity & Assignment*
> *I Am Savvy Strategists Aligning The Practical With The Spiritual*
> *For The Benefit Of All*
> *I Am A Releaser Of Wealth In People And Business*
> *I Am A Bringer Of Hope,*
> *Keeper Of Clarity,*
> *Grower Of Confidence*
> *I Am A King Maker*
> *I Am Brave Leadership Consulting*

Awww sookie sookie now! Isn't she dope? Before Jesus introduced me to Brave's eternal identity, I had been interacting with her as if she were generic and not masterfully crafted by the hands of the Father, fashioned in Jesus and anointed by the Holy Spirit. Once I saw who Brave was in the Spirit, our interactions changed. Based on my personal statement and my business's statement, can't you see why God put us together? He is good, loves me, and loves the clients (internal and external) that we serve. We complement each other so well. But we were both put on Earth to service humanity in a very specific way.

When you know a name, you know a function. Names are important to God because they connote function, ability, and destiny. God changed several people's names to anchor them in His promise. Knowing Brave's Identity has given me so much clarity and confidence as her executive. I step flat-footed into opportunities that I wouldn't have because of the spiritual foundation upon which I stand.

I understand Brave's boundaries and boundaries are good. Jesus had boundaries on Earth for His ministry, not because He was restricted but rather because He needed to be preserved. If you've ever eaten or seen an Egg McMuffin from McDonald's, you know that the freshly cracked egg always fits the size of the English muffin. Why? Because the egg is cracked in a tin mold that ensures a consistent shape for the muffin. In other words, boundaries keep you fit for where you are supposed to go. We all have great favor, anointing, wisdom, power, and demonstration but there are certain times, places, and with certain groups and messages that favor, wisdom, power, and demonstration is strongest. Understanding your business identity will easily help you discern what is aligned to you and what is not, so you can then leverage your identity for product development, sales, marketing, hiring etc.

Like me on the phone with that boy's father, too many Christian business owners, founders, CEOs and leaders are stumbling through, losing our royal eloquence and governmental standing in business because we have not consulted the One who created our business, and by extension, our business's eternal identity in Heaven. Instead we try to devise deeper understanding by diving into understanding why, manifesting, mindfulness, abundance, and intentionality. We set marketing plans, sales projections, product development, branding campaigns, investment deals, etc. without knowledge of who the business is. We try to attract customers, grants, funding and opportunities based on internal and external identities that sound good but have no spiritual authority. And when something works because we accidentally stumbled into it, two things get the credit. Either credit goes to luck, favor, or the blessing of the Lord because we have no clue why it worked and we aren't about to question it. Or credit goes to hard work, clarity, intentionality, a rocking morning routine, a bomb diggity bomb bomb list of affirmations, manifesting, good stewardship, our gratitude journal, consistency, our never-give-up attitude, our killer funnel, webinar, email marketing, speech or a host of other tools we use in life and business.

Your business's identity in Heaven is critical to your business's success. I don't care if you have multiple businesses; each of them has an identity. The more you have, the more important it is to know their identities so you know which one is talking to you, or which one God is giving directives on. I am convinced you will not reach your business's fullest destiny without knowing its identity and knowing it well.

HOW TO IDENTIFY YOUR BUSINESS IDENTITY

At this point the obvious question is, how do I know my business's identity? Before I go there, let me say this. Please do not elevate the statement above listening to Jesus. The identity statement is a tool to help you understand how to co-create and conquer on earth to expand the Kingdom. It is not to replace your relationship with Jesus but to spark it in a different way. Okay, back to the question. How do you identify your business's identity in Heaven? Take a wild guess. If you guessed through prayer, then you are correct! You engage in TALK ♦ ASK ♦ LISTEN™. The beauty of the Kingdom Prayer Framework is that it works whether you are using it alone or in a collective setting. Imagine what could happen if the entire C-suite or board of the company took some time to engage in TALK ♦ ASK ♦ LISTEN™ to hear from Heaven. The beauty of corporate TALK ♦ ASK ♦ LISTEN™ is that each person hears from

Heaven according to the role they play in the organization. Shameless plug: if you need a facilitator to run this collective spiritual engagement for your business or non profit organization, hit me up. I'm really good at this because it is part of Brave's identity to do this for you. That's why I provide Business Identity Consulting services. Businesses speak to me. It's not some prophetic party trick. I serve as a facilitator and guide in co-creating with you, Heaven, and the business in crafting the statement that best describes your business in Heaven. I've trained my ear to hear the wisdom, strategies and insight from Heaven held for them and how to practically release them on earth. It's so fun. I have conducted numerous sessions with business owners, and the results are always the same: a tidal wave of clarity and confirmation in what they need next. In Chapter 7, I give more case study receipts on how businesses and individuals used parts of the Kingdom Prayer Framework for business success. Reach out to see if you qualify for the service by visiting www.BraveLeadershipConsulting.com.

How can you use the TALK ♦ ASK ♦ LISTEN™ parts of the framework to identify a business's identity? There are a couple of ways you can do it. You can ASK outright, "who is my business in heaven?" then write down everything He says. Ta da! Done. I recognize that for some of you, this may not be the easiest because most business owners are not used to hearing from God in this way. Concerns about doing it "right" can get you stuck in your head questioning what you heard, especially if it doesn't make sense. If you don't book a Business Identity session with me, then here are a few ASK prompts to get the conversation going:

- What is the reason and purpose for my business?
- What do customers experience when they interact with us?
- What do we do really well by accident or without effort?
- How does our biggest challenge point to our greatest solution?
- What is the great desire in Your heart concerning us?

On your end, identify what products and services are the most impactful and which ones sold the best. ASK why? What do they have in common? Ask Holy Spirit to highlight the commonality between your products and services. Write down the words people use to describe the results they have experienced through your business. What do they say? Review testimonials. Go deeper than the generic words. Write all of it down and see if there is a certain phrasing that you hear all the time.

- Based on all the intel you gather, put it into 5-6 "I am" statements as if the business is declaring itself to the world.
- Tweak the sentences until it resonates in your toes.

Before I do any advisory work with a business, the first thing we do is craft their Business Identity statement. It's non-negotiable. Why? Because although I call myself an Executive Advisor or Business Advisor, my first and most important responsibility is to be an ear and mouthpiece for Heaven. I cannot and will not advise unless I can hear what God is saying for a business. This doesn't mean you take my word as gold. I have a whole protocol for helping Executives judge what they hear, even what they hear from me or my team. Your business identity statement lets me understand the measure of the business's rules. Second Corinthians 10:13 says, *"We will not boast about what lies outside the area of work which God has given us; rather, we will boast within our assigned area, and that area does reach as far as you."* (CJB)

The way we teach business, in the US at least, is that it is the norm for businesses to fail and abnormal for businesses to succeed. Long ago, my Small Business Association business coach said that 8 out 10 businesses fail within the first 5 years so don't feel bad if this doesn't work out. Fast forward ten years, as I survey the landscape, I had some TALK ♦ ASK ♦ LISTEN™ around what I saw. I saw good businesses go out of business too often. Then God said, *Yeah, that's illegal.* In Heaven, it is illegal for business to fail at the rate they do when keys to success are spiritually available. Even though it is illegal, it still happens. Yes, some businesses are not meant to last forever. They have a fixed end point. That is not the same as failing.

As a business owner, how do you expect to market, create products or services, hire, and fulfill when you don't know the spiritual and physical bounds of your assignment?

LEVERAGING YOUR IDENTITY FOR PROFITABILITY

Once you have the Business Identity, what do you do with it? You thread everything through it. Once I had my identity statement, I rewrote our company mission, vision, and values statements. Then I made a list of every product or service that Brave ever offered into two categories, hits and misses. I compared both lists against her identity statement. Sure enough, EVERY single product or service we offered that aligned to her identity was in the hit column… even if it was something I offered briefly or didn't offer it any more. I could make the connection. I ASKed about the misses column, and Holy Spirit walked me line by line about why that product missed. The main reason was it was outside our boundaries. For instance, way back in the day, I tried offering life coaching services. That bombed big time, and I am so glad it did. My lane was business, and helping people have better relationships with their kids, friends, siblings, and all that drained me so much. But when people asked about their career, it fired me up, and my skills and wisdom kicked up a notch whenever it was business related. It kicked up even more when it was leader and leadership related.

I had one of my clients do this exercise after her business identity session. She came to me because she had two specific problems. The first was she had trouble filling a key position on her team. She recently let the last person go and felt like she was wasting money. The second problem was she needed clarity on what project to focus on for the next quarter. All of her normal means of discovering this solution weren't working. Before we jumped in, I had her do this hit or miss exercise, but with a twist. I love operating in the prophetic because you can have a framework, but the Holy Spirit will say to tweak it this way this time, and it opens new ideas. The twist on the assignment: I've never used it again, but the result was she saw why she was having a hard time keeping a person in that position and ended up saving over $80,000 in salary and benefits. The other result pointed to a project that she put on the back shelf and that had $15 million in contracts attached to it. I will never forget her session. Her business was bold to push forward this project in the session. As its executive, she heard God loud and clear and was off to the races.

If you can't match a product or service offering to an identity statement, then don't sell it until you can. *But Julia, I sell physical products. My candles, t-shirts, and jewelry can't align to a statement.* Yes, they can. It just may not be direct. I worked with a woman in direct sales. She didn't *own* the products she sold, but she did own the business under which her independent distributorship operated. She tied her product to the identity statements and differentiated herself from all the others selling the same product by using the messaging of her identity statement. I have worked with companies in so many different industries that I can craft a profitable connection to anything.

> *"Train up a child in the way they should go. And when he is old he will not depart from it."* (Proverbs 22:6 NKJV)

Who determines the way the child should go? The parents do not determine the way the child should go; God determines the way the child should go. It is the parent's job to connect with God to understand what He placed in that child, then eventually show the child how to connect with God so He can train her/him up in the way they should go.

I see my business the same way. When you wrap your mind around your business identity, you are connecting with the mind of God about what He intended for your business in the first place. You will then see how your business fits into God's plan to establish a family, establish a government, and expand both. You will see how your business fits His intent and to reach, to create wealth. I am here to empower and equip people to dominate their assignment. With your business identity, you will have a guidepost for every product or service you develop.

Maybe the ideas for your business are flowing so quickly that you cannot keep track of what your next assignment is. In that case, return to your business identity and compare the idea against the identity statement. If you cannot figure out how it fits, then that is not something to pursue. Maybe it will fit later on, and right now maybe He is just dropping the seed in your soil, and five years from now or five months from now you will get a revelation about how that new idea or product actually fits into the identity of the company. Or for those of whose business it is to grow businesses, it might be an idea for a client.

Whatever the case, you can sell with confidence knowing that you didn't make something up but you co-created it with God. It takes R& D to a whole other level. You can sell products with confidence knowing that your product is backed by Heaven. When you pray this way, it is not manipulating God because this is what Heaven says you are supposed to be doing.

Setbacks and failures are merely tools of refinement and are to be welcomed instead of dreaded. What did the setback teach you about refining your process? Look at your flops and your failures as things that are preparing you and equipping you for what is coming next.

Some of you have statements and missions that work beautifully, which is wonderful. You can also look back and see the things that hurt your heart, when you put all the time and money and effort into making something magnificent but it did not even garner the attention of those you marketed to. Those were moments of refinement, a place where you learned what to do and what not to do. Praying the Kingdom way will help you begin to see territories and kingdoms in the way God sees them.

You will begin to see things from a heavenly perspective instead of through the lens of corruption. Then you can begin to pray and call those things back into redemption and right standing with the Lord. Get ready for insights on how to better execute your own business because of this framework.

Pray the Kingdom Way Prayer Prompt #5: *Most of you think the practical application is to go ask God for your business identity statement, and that is certainly on the list. However, I would rather you find a business or a brand that you are familiar with and ask God about the reason and purpose for that brand or business. Maybe it's your favorite grocery store, restaurant, or clothing retailer. When you choose another brand or business about which to question God, it takes the pressure off and becomes a great way to practice hearing what the Lord is saying. Pick a business and write a three-sentence business identity statement. TALK ♦ ASK ♦ LISTEN™ to Holy Spirit on behalf of that business. What does Heaven say?*

CHAPTER 6

THE PURPOSE OF MONEY IN THE KINGDOM

REASON AND PURPOSE FOR MONEY

This is probably my favorite chapter in the whole book. I had to lay the foundation of a good and loving God being the creator of all things and having a reason and purpose for everything just so I could get you to accept some of the money truths I'm going to share here. Most of us have been brought up with a poverty or lack mentality when it comes to money. In our attempts not to be accused of loving money because loving it is the root of all evil and junk, we've done a major disservice to the true idea of money. We must shift our view of money from the people who did malice with it to God's view when He created it.

> *"All things were made through Him, and without Him nothing was made that was made."* (John 1:3 NKJV)

Money is a created thing, and Jesus is supreme over all creation, so anything that has been created, money included, came through Jesus first. Jesus has the ultimate understanding and idea of how money should function. As a Kingdom minded entrepreneur, business owner, or business leader, it is important to have the perspective of the One who created and the One for which it was created. I have heard many people say that money is just a tool. I disagree. **Money isn't just a tool; it is God's tool.** That makes a difference. A hammer is a human tool and can be used any way a human wants. A hammer is not a tool for dogs or flowers or insects. Money is a created thing and as such, God gets to say what its reason and purpose is. This is why Jesus preached so much about money's proper uses. Give it to the poor, not to make a political or social system out of helping orphans and widows, but because it was created to provide for their needs. Money is to be sown or invested to reap a crop and interest because it too was designed to reproduce after its own kind. Business is the only system that allows money to reproduce after its own kind to the degree that all the people of the world can be blessed. Money is to be used for needs and wants.

I began asking God about the reason and purpose for money. *The reason money exists is to reflect God's desire to permeate all things.* What does the word *permeate* mean? Permeate means to infuse, to be in all of it.

> *"Another parable He spoke to them: 'The Kingdom of heaven is like leaven, which a woman took and hid in three measures of meal till it was all leavened.'"* (Matthew 13:33 NKJV)

> *"And again, He said, 'To what shall I liken the Kingdom of God? It is like leaven, which a woman took and hid in three measures of meal till it was all leavened.'"* (Luke 13:20-21 NKJV)

When questioned about the Kingdom, Jesus spoke in parables to explain to his followers that yeast is used in making bread. Even though one only needs a tiny bit of yeast in the flour, it permeates every part of the dough. As you come into Kingdom understanding, the Kingdom will begin to permeate every area of your life.

Money exists to reflect the heart of God and God's desire to permeate all things. The **purpose of money is provision. Its function is to provide for all things.**

> *"A feast is made for laughter, and wine makes merry; but money answers everything."* (Ecclesiastes 10:19 NKJV)

Have you ever heard that scripture and wondered what it meant? It does not mean that you can throw money at everything, but it does mean that it is a provision for all things. Try to consider anything in the lives of humans that money does not affect, and you will find there is nothing that money does not affect. Money permeates everything; there is nothing money does not touch. If there is too much of it, it is called surplus or excess. If there is too little, it is called deficit and lack.

I have heard people say that money is neutral, that it is neither good nor bad. Not true. Money is not nor has it ever been neutral. **Money is good because God created it, and everything God created was good.** Not only is money good, but money has a preference, a bias if you will, toward God. It prefers God. It desires to be used for Kingdom things. It recognizes its creator and, if I may continue to personify it for the sake of this point, prefers to be used according to its function, for His good. In Romans 8: 19-23, the scripture says all creation groans waiting for the sons of God to be revealed. The reason for their revealing is so the sons of God can free creation from the curse. This shows us two things: (1) That creation has an affinity for its creator and (2) that creation recognizes its ruler. Throughout the Bible, created things recognized and responded to God. In the Old Testament, the ram in the bush, the ravens that fed Elijah, and the bear that killed the prophet's mockers are all examples. In the New Testament, created things respond to Jesus or angels: Balaam's donkey, the axehead that floated, the fish with the coin in its mouth, water that turned into wine, and the turbulent wind and waves are just a few examples. The spirit world interacts with everything according to who it is and what its function is. Why is it important to see money not only as God's tool but also that money prefers to do the things of God? Because as it permeates and provides, it shows all how glorious God is. When Sheba saw Solomon's wealth and abundance, she didn't say, "Homie has it going on." No! It says in 1 King 10:9 that she praised his God. She saw his wisdom and riches and praised God. Money operating in its function shows people God's care and provision. When you see the proper use of the thing God made, it points back to proper relationship and connection with a good and loving Father and draws us closer to Him.

Yes, big business, Wall Street, governments, credit card companies, banks, corporations, scammers, and schemers have given money a bad rap. However, we, the sons/daughters of God who were created to have dominion over the Earth. Instead of redeeming money, we have accepted and agreed with the current atmosphere and climate over money and keep it in further bondage.

My friend and team member Ingrid and I were practicing TALK for a client who had about $200,000 being held up for a major project. We gathered to collectively gain some prophetic insight regarding this situation. As we conversed, I saw a vision. I saw cartoon money in all types of denominations dancing and vibrating with excitement. Then it began to speak to me.

"Release us," it said.

I was so confused.

"What?" I questioned.

"Release us. We want to partner with this Kingdom work, so release us to do so."

"Ok, you are released," I said. Then I saw this great valley filled with these dancing bills rise to the air and catch a jet current and flow away really quickly. I told Ingrid all about it, and then she said she saw dancing plates, and the lyrics from *Be Our Guest* from Beauty and the Beast popped in my head. I opened the laptop to go view the lyrics because… you know… God speaks to me through lyrics. I got the sense I was supposed to verbally welcome money. As I was doing so, I heard money say, *"We're not welcome."*

"What do you mean? Everyone wants money," I replied.

"Yeah, but we're not welcome. We're partners in Kingdom work, and the people we want to partner with don't want us," it said.

There was a lyric in the song that said, *Life is so unnerving for a servant who's not serving.* The conversation went deeper from there. I have a whole video about the encounter where I share the full depth of the revelation and conversation in my Pray The Kingdom Way online course. I was flabbergasted. Why? Because it never occurred to me that all *things pertaining to life and godliness* talked about in 2 Peter 1:3 were waiting to interact with me. It was like we were seated at the boardroom table in Heaven with Jesus, Father, and Holy Spirit, and on the agenda was a guest speaker, and that speaker was money. It was given the floor and got to plead its case. Although it wasn't the first time I had a conversation with money, it was most certainly the most in-depth one up until that point. Ingrid and I TALKed to God about what we heard money say. As a feeler, I distinctly remember feeling like my friend was sad, like we'd hurt its feelings without knowing it. I tested what I heard against scripture and wise counsel for months afterwards, just digging in. It wasn't a revelation that I shared immediately. I needed to test and judge the word. So I did.

This is why the "attack" on money is so great in the church. If the Kingdom redeemers of money are convinced that the thing we're to redeem is horrible, dirty, nasty, and evil, then we continue to subject money to be used in cursed and wicked things. God said to me, *"I hate sex trafficking, but instead of my kids gaining wealth, they are fighting over the piety of staying poor."* All of the humans behind the illegal and immoral ways money is being circulated are doing so partly because Kingdom people have not adopted God's reason and purpose for money. How can we bring the atmosphere of Heaven to Earth when we already agree with the atmosphere of money currently here? That math ain't mathing.

This is why greed, hoarding, and being miserly is terrible. It doesn't reflect the heart of money's creator. Nowhere in Heaven is one part plush and the other depraved. The climate of Heaven is abundant and overflowing. This is why the master called the servant with the talents wicked because even if the master was harsh, with a proper understanding of money, the servant could have redeemed the reputation of the master with the good work of his money if the servant adopted the Kingdom view. I used to think the reason the master gave the one with ten talents more was steeped in the adage of the rich getting richer and the poor getting poorer. But what if it's not? What if it is solely based on understanding the function of money and it flows to those who understand how to make it move?

THE LAW OF CIRCULATION

Stagnant water stinks. Without a flow coming in and going out, there is no sustainability. Why? Because it is not moving. It is not going anywhere. This principle can be used for our own bodies as well. Our hearts have right and left ventricles that move the blood in our bodies through the heart to be oxygenated and then circulated throughout our bodies. When there is no input and/or output in a body of water, the body of water eventually goes stagnant, then dries up. The law of circulation must be in play to avoid stagnation.

> *"Give, and it will be given to you: good measure, pressed down, shaken together, and running over will be put into your bosom. For with the same measure that you use, it will be measured back to you."* (Luke 6:38 NKJV)

> *"Do not be deceived, God is not mocked; for whatever a man sows, that he will also reap."* (Galatians 6:7 NKJV)

God is in the circulation business and in the business of exchange. Money is a *currency* because currents flow. We have the stock *exchange* because shares are traded, going out with a sale, and coming in with a purchase. Buying and selling is a part of the law of circulation. Money must move, and business is the vehicle for unlimited money circulation. By the way, that client we released money over called to tell us the $200k had been released.

Why do Kingdom business owners fear setting the right price and fear sales? Because sales invite you to the law of circulation and exchange. Many Kingdom business owners are afraid of the exchange and are stuck in their pricing structure, undercharging for their services based on fear. The correct price point for your business does not have to be cheap. It takes the same energy to sell your product for one dollar as it does to sell it for one million dollars. The price point is not the point. The price point is whatever price you choose based on your target market. What is the true value of what you are offering? Again, business is the vehicle for unlimited money circulation.

"Charge what you are worth" is a saying that is very popular in these internet streets. You are priceless, so you cannot charge what you are worth. That puts a price tag on you. Do not charge what you are worth; instead, determine the rate of exchange for your service or product. You become better when people pay you more. The price is the price, and there is a purpose that it serves. Consider your business, what God has called you to do, and the impact you are supposed to make. If you would not pay the charged amount for your services, it's because you are not your ideal client. Your cousin, mom, and brother are not your ideal client either, especially for the level of vision in your heart. Listen. Release the hurt that they didn't buy from you, and go find your true people.

ELEVEN SPIRITUAL FACTS ABOUT MONEY

1. *Money needs purpose*. When money has a Kingdom purpose, it garners attention and stays in alignment. It requires a demand on the anointing, a hunger, and a desire for fulfillment. If you are saying to yourself that you need to see the money before you pay for something, then ask God about that. There are times in business when you have to move forward before the money is present. When I made my first hire,

I did not have the money to do so. The Lord told me that the moment I made the hire, I would be placing my demand and giving money purpose. I have not once missed a payroll.

2. *Money likes to move.* Part of the reason why hoarding money is so horrible is because the hoarder is actually preventing money from doing what it was designed to do, which is to move. In the law of circulation, there must be a flow of money moving in and out. If money is coming in, and it has nowhere to go, it will become stagnant. This is why you have feast and famine cycles in business. Products and services are the legal way money flows into your business. If you have nothing to sell, money can't move. If you have no income, you can't give, grow, or sustain wealth.

3. *Money was designed to reproduce after its own kind.* When God created the garden and all the seed-bearing life, everything in the garden was able to produce after its own kind. Plants, vegetation, animals, and insects have 'seeds' for this very reason, to reproduce. Technology even begets technology. We see this in the parable of the talents.

> *26 "But his lord answered and said to him, 'You wicked and lazy servant, you knew that I reap where I have not sown, and gather where I have not scattered seed. 27 So you ought to have deposited my money with the bankers, and at my coming I would have received back my own with interest. 28 So take the talent from him, and give it to him who has ten talents."* (Matthew 25:14-28 NKJV)

Part of the reason the man was considered wicked was because he did not let the money reproduce after its own kind.

4. *Money is a servant of mankind and a partner in the Kingdom.* Money is not a master; money is a servant. What I mean by servant is that money is in partnership with what God intends to do on the earth.

You cannot have a dictator relationship with money; money is not your slave. Jesus had a right relationship with everything. The relationship that you have with money must be one that allows it to grow, one that is of respect, and one that sees it for its function.

5. *Money speaks.* Money has a way of communicating what is valuable.

> *"For where your treasure is, there your heart will be also."* (Matthew 6:21 NKJV)

Money speaks where you spend it. How you interact with money, how you treat money, will speak to what you value. Consider art at an exhibit. There may be two very similar paintings hanging next to one another on the wall. You see that it is quite difficult to tell them apart. One painting is priced at $100, the other at $1,000. Which one carries the most value? Which one speaks to you? Money communicates to you what you value.

6. *Money is good.* We already talked about this. God created it, so it is good. We need to understand how to flow it towards the assignments to reflect its God-given goodness.

7. *Money moves on behalf of those who have it.* If someone is using money for illegal purposes, then money will take on sinful nature. But money in the hands of a believer will take on a nature of righteousness and be used to glorify God and advance the Kingdom on Earth. In 2017, a private equity group purchased two parks from the City of Memphis, TN. Why? Because all legal recourse to remove two Confederate statues of General Nathan Bedford Forrest, founder of the Ku Klux Klan and Confederate President, Jefferson Davis, had failed. With the property under private ownership, the owners had the legal right to remove the statues.

8. *Money needs direction and management.* Direction and management are why your spending dollars are so important. If you do not have bank accounts and a budget, then you will have no direction. You are solely in charge of directing and managing the inflow and outflow of your cash reserves. What bookkeeping software are you using? What accounting systems are you using? Businesses should have places to direct and manage money toward savings, taxes, operating expenses, and payroll.

9. *Money is a gatherer.* Have you noticed that people gather according to their social-economical stances? It is important for you to have people around you who are gathering money the way you see yourself gathering money. People who are in lack gather together. People who are financially blessed gather together. Which room are you in currently? Money exists in abundance. God is excessive; there is plenty to go around, and I want every penny that has been assigned to me. We must stop thinking that money is evil; that thought has us rejecting it, and those mindsets stop the law of circulation. If all you ever desire to do is give, and someone tries to give to you, you are not able to receive, and the viability of that transaction dies. If all you ever do is receive, but never give and allow money to flow, the viability will die.

10. *Money is limited by its possessor's belief.* If there is some part of you that thinks having money is bad, you will always intuitively reject all forms of financial advancement. In his course, Wealth With God, Jim Baker, not the 80s dude, answers the question *how much money is too much?* this way. Any amount of money that takes you away from trusting God is too much. Your relationship with money shows who is Lord of your life.

> *"No one can serve two masters; for either he will hate the one and love the other, or else he will be loyal to the one and despise the other. You cannot serve God and mammon." (Matthew 6:24 NKJV)*

He goes on to say that the spirit of mammon is the part of you that thinks you need to be in control and tighten the straps so you can be a good steward, but the fact is you are just being cheap. Being cheap and being a good steward are not the same. To be a good steward of money, you must understand its reason and purpose, then train it up in the way it should interact with your business. Many have been trained on money as a consumer but have not been trained on money as a business owner. Your Lord is whoever you have to consult before you do what God tells you to do. If you must consult your bank account before doing what God tells you to do, then money is your Lord. What about making good, sound financial decisions? Yes, make good, sound financial decisions, but do not make those decisions out of a place of fear.

11. Money is an accelerator. The timing of God is important. And in the timing of God, money functions as an accelerator to achievement. You can learn to do *anything* for free these days. If you want to shed a few pounds, you do not need money to do so. You can Google diets and exercise plans for free. You don't need a gym membership or any equipment at all to reach your goal. You can DIY it and reach your goal. Just know that if you don't spend money, you will spend time. If you have money for a personal trainer, nutritionist, therapist, and home chef, you will accelerate your results. You can build an addition to your house by yourself, but your results will be accelerated by hiring a contractor and crew. I saw this so profoundly in a sermon my pastor preached on a topic that had nothing to do with money. One of the scriptures he used arrested me. We're familiar with the story of the prodigal son in Luke 15. The son got his inheritance from his father, went wild'n out, and then after getting his butt kicked by his choices, decided to come back home. In verse 17-18 in the NIV it says *"When he came to his senses, he said 'How many of my father's hired servants have food to spare, and here I am starving to death! I will set out and go back to my father..."* Isn't it interesting that the thing that made the son "come to his senses" was NOT his father's provision but the provision of the servants? Think about this. According to verse 14, the whole country was in a famine. The son had a need. But shame and guilt kept him from returning home as his rightful position as a son. Instead, it was the provision of the servants. His father's employees had food to spare. The employees had excess. The employees were so well provided for that it stirred envy in the heart of the son to desire to be in a similar state. In other words, the money of the employees accelerated his return home. His father had to be wealthy in order to be able to give his son his inheritance money in the first place. That meant that His father was likely in business. The Kingdom's purpose of business is to create wealth to take care of all people. The purpose of money is provision. We see that in operation here. In a time of famine, the Kingdom purpose of business and money was operating so well in the father's life that he could throw a party (a display of excess) for the son after he returned. It is powerful enough to know that it was the money of the father's employees that accelerated the son's return. But what really got me was thinking about what would have happened if the opposite was true. What if the son's father was broke? How much longer would the son have stayed away? When the son wouldn't return because of love, he returned because of money. The provision he needed was at home in his father's house. How many sons and daughters would have recovered from addiction sooner, if they had money for the program that worked the best? How many would have had greater education if the money was available for books, equipment, or tutors?

Too many Christian business owners, too many Kingdom-minded people are trying to manage money without a revelation of what money is designed to do in the Kingdom. They tip toe around it hoping not to disappoint God or lose their soul. Money is designed to flow. It is designed to permeate all areas. Because what I put my money to and wherever money is being generated, God can touch. That is why it is everywhere and is a legal access point for the Kingdom. Your money mindset is shaped by your parents, your culture, television, movies, media, and your experiences. If you have continued to believe that Jesus was poor, then you have exalted poverty to a place of lordship. What if God wants to make you an example of what righteousness looks like while living in excess? Money is a created thing, and in the Kingdom, we need to teach created things how to function properly. If business is a vehicle for unlimited money circulation, and if the reason God created money was to reflect His desire to permeate all things and provide for all things, then why do you accept lack?

INVITING MONEY

Inviting money into your business is not hard. You can do it in the spirit. A great ASK prompt: *How can I make more money in my business in the next 90 days?* And there are also some practical things you can do too. Here's a list of some obvious and often overlooked ways to invite money.

- Get your business license
- Create product and services
- Forgive yourself and others
- Market and sell something
- Advertise
- Pay your bills on time
- Stay current with your taxes
- Hire
- Upgrade equipment or systems
- Give it a purpose and direction
- Give
- Invest
- Express gratitude

Money Healing Exercise (optional): *Write a letter to money admitting all the wrong ways in which you have viewed it. Start from the very first thing that you remember your parents saying to you or in front of you that influenced how you see money. Start there. Is there something within your ethnic culture that is keeping* *you in bondage to old mindsets regarding money and finance? What are all the ways you thought about it?*

After you write the letter, I want you to burn it as a sign to you that on that day you are changing the script.

Next, write a new letter to money outlining how you will pursue a right relationship moving forward. TALK to God, ASK, then LISTEN. What does a right relationship with money look like for you and your business?

Money has permission, and it permeates. You do not need all the money in the world. You just need all the money that is connected to your world. It is not enough to say that you receive it. Your mindset shift and your new habits will create a welcoming atmosphere for growth opportunities. Some of us need to grow up in our relationship with money. In order to steward the levels to which God is calling you, you need to have a mature attitude about it. It is time to have boardroom conversations with finance and Kingdom wealth. Transformation happens when you Pray The Kingdom Way over your financial situation. It should not be a burden to you. God wants to introduce you to a new concept so that He can change your mind. And if He can change your mind, then He can change your actions. Moses did not ask to be the deliverer; he was called to do it. Some of you are called to steward excessive amounts of money, and you keep saying, *"No, God. I don't know anyone who's doing that. What if I make a mistake? What if I invest in the wrong thing?"* If you take the mindset that because you did not see a return on an investment before, you refuse to invest in anything else, then that is incorrect thinking. I can guarantee you that a return on obedience is greater than a return on investment. If God tells you to do it, He will bless your obedience. After I racked up over $25,000 in credit card debt investing in my business because God told me to invest it, even when it did not make sense to anyone on Earth, I heard from the Lord about freedom from the fear of money. He then told me that I would never have to worry about money again, and in the year of the COVID pandemic, I paid off three credit cards and my vehicle.

Either this works or it does not. Are you going to walk with God to figure out how it works for you? No one can tell you that, and that is precisely why I give you the framework. I am here to empower you to step into that new relationship with money and do it bravely. At some point you are going to have to transition and say with confidence, "*My God is able to deliver me from this, but even if He does not, I will not bow to poverty. I will not bow to lack. I will not bow to fear of growing this business. I will not be fearful of being alone. I know that there are people who are waiting to be my client, friend, investor, or partner at this next level. I know that there are people, things, and communities who are waiting for me. There is a change that is coming, and I am willing to go through what I must go through to get to that place. I do not know where I am going, but I know I cannot stay here. My feet have to move.*"

You walk in the stability of continuous circulation; everything you need is within you. As a Kingdom entrepreneur, you will eventually come to a place where what happens in the stock market or with the value of the dollar will not influence your emotions. Greater is He that is in you, so you have the capacity and the ability to unleash and manifest financial blessing into the world.

Pray the Kingdom Way Prayer Prompt #6: *What is one view of money that I have that you want me to change?*

CHAPTER 7

HOW TO UNAPOLOGETICALLY PRAY FOR PROFITS INTO YOUR BUSINESS

Most business owners agree that profit is best. I am unwavering in this: it is the will of God for Kingdom businesses to operate in profit. At this point in the book, I hope you believe this, too. Operating in profit requires the right financial ecosystem. In this section, I draw on scripture about a promise to the Israelites found in Exodus 3:8 to illustrate the ecosystem necessary for profit. I'll also share examples of how our consulting and advisory clients used facets of Kingdom Prayer Framework and concepts to advance their businesses.

> *So I have come down to rescue them from the hand of the Egyptians and to bring them up out of that land into a good and spacious land, a land flowing with milk and honey—the home of the Canaanites, Hittites, Amorites, Perizzites, Hivites and Jebusites. (Exodus 3:8 NIV)*

There are over 20 verses in the Bible referring to a promised territory described as flowing with milk and honey. But what does that mean? Have you ever seen a milk river? Or a honey river? I haven't. Are there milk and honey waterfalls? I had some TALK ♦ ASK ♦ LISTEN™ with God about this. It is not a literal flow of milk from the land. However, it spoke to abundance and the abundant conditions that made it possible. In order for a land to flow in milk, it needs milk-producing animals or plants. To sustain those animals, the land must be fertile enough to grow vegetation so that milk producing animals can graze, feed, and reproduce. They needed appropriate shelter, boundaries, and even access to veterinary care. They would need to be bred and thus traded. The milk would need to be harvested, stored, bought, and traded in order for it to "flow" in that land.

Similarly, in order for honey to "flow," there had to be a diversity of foliage and flowering plants for bees to feed on and pollinate. It would need the right sunlight and wind conditions, sources of water for irrigation, and beekeepers to tend the hives for honey to be harvested, stored, bought, and sold. In addition to the honey itself, the production and distribution of products from honey and honeycomb could be used in cooking or healing balms or salves.

The promise of a land flowing with milk and honey is a promise of territory that carries within it a prosperous economic system filled with wealth, opportunity, connections, and ideas to take care of people. Did you catch that? The territory has business within it. It carries everything needed for the people to prosper—not just the Israelites, but all the people their trade reaches.

When we talk about praying for profits, I am going to take the "land of milk and honey" approach to explaining it. I am going to talk about praying for a greater ecosystem that makes profits possible and how to apply the Kingdom.

KINGDOM ECOSYSTEM OF PROFITS

An ecosystem is a community of interacting organisms or elements. Each part of the ecosystem serves a function and is important. The scriptures say it this way in 1 Corinthians 12:14, *For the body does not consist of one member but of many.* **The Kingdom ecosystem of profit includes purpose, people, product, pricing, position, and protection.** It sounds like a lot. But you don't have to figure all this out in one day or even one year. As businesspeople, we have to resist our urge to run headlong into the wind because we're so excited. Walk with God and follow His timing. If you are finding yourself stressed with implementing everything, that is a sign that you need to do some TALK ♦ ASK ♦ LISTEN™ to understand what is most important.

PURPOSE

I will always ask God what His reason and purpose is before beginning advisory work with a client. Remember, purpose is the function for which something is created. *What is Your intent for this?* is one of my favorite ASK prompts. The scriptures tell us to seek the Kingdom first, but no one ever told us what that looked like practically. Asking this is how you seek the Kingdom first. The TALK and ASK part of the framework is how you seek the Kingdom first. Getting Heaven's perspective is the easiest way to see *His will be done on Earth as it is Heaven.*

CASE STUDY: Our client, a veterinarian, came to us as she transitioned from working as a W2 to being a full-time entrepreneur and wanted prophetic insight into what was next for her. Using the parts of the Kingdom Prayer Framework, we crafted her business identity statement that gave her the spiritual foundation for the practical moves she needed to make next. The result was she had her first $1,000,000 year. Why? She partnered with God's intent for her business and with her to navigate her transition. She then operated according to that intent.

CASE STUDY: One of my clients came to me because she wanted to be the first woman to be appointed by the President to the highest law enforcement position in her state. I told her immediately that I had zero experience in political campaigns and encouraged her to find someone else. Her reason for coming to me wasn't for my depth of political campaign knowledge but because she wanted to be aligned to her purpose in doing it. She wanted to conduct herself in a way that aligned to her purpose and why she wanted the job regardless of whether she was appointed or not. She knew this assignment was bigger than her. I engaged in the Kingdom Prayer Framework to see if this was even something I was supposed to take on. I got the green light. The strategy we came up with was centered around making connections with sponsors who would offer her name to be on the short list of appointees. Her networking efforts were so drenched in purpose that even though the schedule was daunting, she never felt drained. She made genuine connections in complete integrity. Though she was not appointed, she told me that the process of connecting with higher level government officials positioned her for other opportunities. She leaned into purpose, received strategies that aligned to her integrity and purpose, and was the better for it.

Purpose is an element in the Kingdom Ecosystem of Profits because it aligns you to what God is already doing, thus reducing friction, and backing your efforts because they are His agenda.

PEOPLE

In the Kingdom, *people* are most important. Why? Because people were the only creatures created in the image of God. We were given dominion here on Earth. The Kingdom purpose of business is to create wealth to take care of *people*. People come in many categories:

- Customers
- Employees
- Contractors
- Investors
- Vendors
- Shareholders
- Partners
- Mentors
- Coaches

One of the most overlooked "people" in the people category for a lot of business owners and leaders is the leader. Much of leadership and business development is focused on knowing your customer and taking care of our people. That's important. But so many I work with are taking care of others to the detriment of themselves. I don't work with ego maniacs. I tend to work with people who give too much out of a misplaced sense of piety. It ranges from mild neglect to full blown self-abuse. They are masking their self-abuse under the guise of being selfless, or being a servant leader.

CASE STUDY: One of my clients—we'll call her Gina for the sake of the story—was an employee at an academic institution and had recently been promoted. The institution wanted to promote from within and the choice was between Gina and another coworker on her team. When Gina got the promotion, there was resentment from the coworker who was now her subordinate. The subordinate made derogatory remarks about Gina to other team members, even publicly in team meetings. I asked her why she allowed this behavior. Her reply was that she was "taking the high road" and "wasn't going to dignify her with a response." She admitted, though, that she was thinking about firing her for insubordination. We engaged the Kingdom Prayer Framework to seek a strategy. God was very clear that the strategy He wanted was one that would honor Gina AND the employee. Since honoring

> *people was on God's mind, I had Gina list all the things her new employee was good at. This helped Gina see the gold in a person that wasn't acting so golden. We also spent some time dealing with Gina's own guilt for having been promoted and her pattern of enduring mistreatment. Then we practiced what Gina would say when the employee openly criticized her in their staff meetings. The opportunity presented itself, and Gina used one of her newly minted power statements that showed honor to the employee and honor Gina. I'll never forget her voice when she called me and told me how well it went. The righteous strategy produced righteous results. The employee was invited to change her behavior and did because God said the strategy for them was honor. Gina grew in her leadership skills as well. They ended up having an amazing relationship after that.*

It is easy to read that case study and get fixated on the breakdown of the power statement we practiced. But the statement wasn't the point. That strategy worked because it aligned with what God was doing in the heart of his people. Based on God's desire, when we choose a tool that best supports His agenda, it works. It produces righteousness, joy, and peace.

> *CASE STUDY: One of my clients owned a special needs after school care facility. She'd outgrown her current space and needed a new building. When she engaged with us, she was pressured by the weight of the assignment. She could serve more families in a bigger facility. Caregiving is taxing, and she had a way of getting through to her special needs kids, some of whom were nonverbal, that amazed parents and workers. She had done her due diligence and had found several options that would work. One in particular was her favorite, and she wanted a strategy. We engaged in*

the Kingdom Prayer Framework and heard an unusual strategy. The solution was that she was to go on vacation. I will never forget her face. It was clear that was not what she was expecting. She resisted at first, but to her credit she did take some time off, and, when she came back, she put in a bid for the property she really wanted. Her bid was rejected. The strategy remained for her to find ways to take time for herself. A while later, she gets a call from the city asking if she still wanted to buy the property. She did, and she got it at a lower price than asking.

In the people section, I didn't share examples about how customers were blessed because of a business. We can find those anywhere. I wanted to highlight that your business or business leadership is just as much a reflection of His love of you as it is of the people who benefit from your products or service. You will not pray unapologetically if you feel like you have to martyr yourself for the sake of your business or customers.

I have seen several movies about Wall Street corruption. The corruption happened because people found a way to degrade, belittle, be dishonest toward, and disregard other people. Because people are an element in the Kingdom Ecosystem of Profits, Kingdom businesses should treat people correctly. This doesn't mean people will always like your product or service or that they'll never complain. It means that your regard for all the people associated with your business, internally and externally, need to be drenched in the Kingdom's way of viewing people, including yourself.

PRODUCT

If people are the most important asset, then every product is to serve a person, whether that is a singular person or a group of people. *What about products that serve pets?* Pets don't purchase; their people do, so the product serves the people who have pets. Every product serves people either by meeting a need, by solving a problem, or satisfying a want.

There are two definitions of products that I want us to look at. The first definition of *product*, according to BusinessDictionary.com, is *a good, an idea, a method, information, object or service created as a result of a process and serves a need or satisfies a want.* The second definition of *product* is *a good or service that closely meets the requirement of a particular market and yields enough profit to justify its continued existence.*

From the first definition, we see that a product can be an idea. If you think about it, leadership is a product that is just an idea. You can't touch, smell, or taste leadership. It is an idea from which we create things. A product can be a method, a way that you do something. The DevaCut® is a method for cutting curly hair.

From the second definition, we see that a product needs to meet the requirement of a particular market AND yield enough profit to justify its continued existence. Proctor and Gamble kept Febreze® in research development for years. Its initial release failed because it didn't meet the requirements of a market. They tried again, and it has sold hundreds of millions. Blockbuster® is an example of a company that did not generate enough profit to justify its existence.

We know from marketing that all products and services must have a combination of tangible and intangible attributes; these are the benefits, features, and functions that we offer to people who are going to buy. It can be tricky identifying what those are or which ones to highlight if you don't seek God.

CASE STUDY: One of my clients was a set of business partners who came together to start a new company. Each was an entrepreneur on their own but sensed God telling them to officially partner together and form a new company. Using parts of the Kingdom Prayer Framework, I helped them craft their new business's identity statement. From there we engaged more in the framework, and they created their first product. ASK prompts included things like, what is the thing our customer recognizes they need? What is the way our customer will receive it? What is the price point that best benefits our company? What clients can easily pay that price? How do we talk about this product that gets our customers' attention? It surprised them because they had something else in mind originally. They later told us that the process of creating products from a spiritual foundation helped them go from idea to test to launch so much faster.

Using the Kingdom Prayer Framework, you get to create products that have practical impact on Earth. The only reason you wouldn't use this framework is because you are believing some lie that's preventing you from believing that you can. *It will take too long.* There is a learning curve, but it doesn't have to be long. Wouldn't it be worth the wait? What would change if you invested the time to learn how to create products that God's longing to release with insight in how to position them in the market?

CASE STUDY: Another set of clients owned a storage facility. The product is inherently set, but when they came to us, they were looking for an internal product. The product they needed was an internal one, a decision method, that allowed them to decide how to find the perfect next property to increase their portfolio of properties. We engaged the Kingdom Prayer Framework to craft the business identity. Immediately, they saw their method. Unbeknownst to us, the identity of the business carried the method. They extracted that method from the statements of their identity and created their property acquisition system. The system allowed them to see not just the numbers but, also the spiritual potential of an offer. Can you imagine that? Having a documented way

> *of seeing the financial and spiritual impact of a property? They implemented this internal product and immediately the stress and fear of wondering if this was a good deal or not melted. It was like they had a secret weapon, created specifically for their business, and it empowered them to engage more intentionally in their business expansion.*

Not all products are external. This was an example of an internal product they created to expand their business. Products give money a legal avenue to flow towards you. Without products, there is no profit. Because products are an element in the Kingdom Ecosystem of Profits, much attention needs to go to producing and refining your products.

PRICING

I tell my clients, there is purpose in every price tag. Pricing is about settling on the rate of exchange for a good or service. The price of a product should include cost to make or fulfill that product and profit margin. It is the intersection of value and cost. The POS is an altar. POS is the point of sale. I don't mean we worship your merchant service account or cash register. In the scriptures, altars are places of exchange. At the altar, I give God ashes; He exchanges it for beauty. I give Him my burden; He exchanges it for peace. I give Him my ignorance; He gives me wisdom. In business, people exchange money in order to meet a need, solve a problem, or satisfy a want.

In her book, *Market Like a Mogul*, Dr. Shamieka Dean says, "[l]owering your prices does not equate to more sales. Your prices should never be affordable. They should be accessible to 'your' audience."[8] Affordability is relative. A Rolls Royce is affordable to a billionaire. Your price reveals a lot about the confidence of the seller. If someone had a brand new

---

[8] (Dean, 2022)

Corvette Stingray for sale for $1, it would immediately spark suspicion. You'd rationalize that it was a toy. Or it was a scam. Or if you're like me, hope it would be like that scene in the *Waiting to Exhale* movie, where Bernadine, played by Angela Bassett, sold her soon-to-be ex-husband's things for $1.

The point is we all have a perceived value of something and will question whenever a price point is higher or lower than our perceived value. Whether positive or negative, pricing will always elicit a response. This is why framing is important. Do you remember those anti-animal cruelty commercials with Sarah McLachlan singing *In the Arms of Angel* in the background? They never just said give $29 a month to help an animal. They framed the price as "for less than a dollar a day" or "for the price of a cup of coffee." This is why the infomercial shows you the ad of a similar product that is more expensive with an X through it. They are price anchoring to elicit a psychological response.

Last year, a television prophet offered an in-person prayer intensive, and church folk lost their minds. Not that she was spending fourteen hours over seven sessions teaching on prayer in person or that there were swag bag goodies. No, the biggest criticism was the $1499.99 price tag to attend. Comedians were going off. I am not here to comment on that product. But know that interactions you see, whether people agree or not, will influence your pricing decisions. If you saw the way people talked dirt about the television prophet, and agreed with them, you may not want to incur that type of criticism for your product and may inadvertently undercharge because of what you believe to be a bad example. This is an instance where you must cast down vain imaginations and every high thing that exalts itself above the knowledge of God. You cannot force God to only do things that will please people. It doesn't work that way. *Praying the Kingdom Way* allows you to check your assumption against what God is instructing in real time and then conform your thoughts to His.

> CASE STUDY: *One of my international clients got the opportunity to pitch a deal to a company in another country. She worked in leadership development and had outlined what the client needed based on the assessment she'd performed. When it came time to price the package, she low balled it. I encouraged her to engage in the Kingdom Prayer Framework to see if God was ok with her pricing. When we spoke next, she told me God was very clear that she needed to raise the price. So she raised the price by $20,000, and she closed the deal.*

Because pricing is an element in the Kingdom Ecosystem of Profits, much attention needs to go to pricing because it directly influences sales and reach.

POSITION

Positioning is about the method of getting people to see your product. How do you position yourself in the market? Marketing terms call this your unique sales proposition. Positioning is the method by which people experience your product. Some of that positioning includes your marketing plan, the platforms where you have reach, offline methods, online methods, et cetera.

> CASE STUDY: *One of my clients, the founder of an online school, had a great product. I could confirm this because I had used it. My client thought the academic depth the school provided could speak for itself. But enrollments were flatlining instead of growing. We engaged in the Kingdom Prayer Framework to craft the identity of the school in Heaven. From there, we sought God about how to position the school in front of its students so the students would be compelled to enroll. The strategy involved getting*

really deep into the mindset of the student. The client used to promote the school by teaching mini lessons. However, that had an unexpected effect. In some TALK ♦ ASK ♦ LISTEN™, God revealed that while people loved the content and were impressed with the teacher's depth of knowledge, they were intimidated by the teacher's eloquence. What the school was purposed to do was empower and equip the students, not impress or intimidate them. So we ASKed what we could do to better position the school in a less intimidating way. The solution was a change in how the teacher taught in promotions. Instead of giving snippets of the content, the focus shifted to building the confidence of the students to change the world. The focus shifted from the content to what the content would allow them to do—change the world in a way that was uniquely them. I helped the client come up with a strategy for presenting that was aligned with this new shift and position the school as the place to go to be equipped in confidence. The result was over $80,000 worth of tuition within a week of the promo event.

The product was very good, but we wouldn't have known that the client was misaligned without applying the Kingdom Prayer Framework.

CASE STUDY: Another client was an author who wrote a fabulous book that got her invitations to speak on many stages. She knew there was a bigger platform out there, but she didn't know where. She used the Kingdom Prayer Framework to craft a powerful decree. Part of it said that she would be known by influencers, and they would seek her out. One day, she hit me up saying her decree got her booked on Gwyneth Paltrow's Goop podcast to be interviewed by Gwyneth Paltrow herself. She told me she knew she was ready to step into the bigger stage because she'd been

> *professing her decree. So when the opportunity presented itself she wasn't "shocked" that God did it, nor did she have to "pray on it" before deciding to do it. She co-created this opportunity in Heaven with God and patiently waited until it showed up on Earth and then stepped in.*

This client didn't use the elements of the framework to seek out an opportunity. She stood flat footed and called it to her. So dope!

> *CASE STUDY: Another client who used the Kingdom Prayer Framework was a W2 employee. He worked at a tech company very autonomously and had great relationships with his bosses. In one project, he needed to pitch to a newly hired senior manager to approve a budget for the next stage of a project already in progress. The senior manager didn't respond to my client in the way he was accustomed to. He was very frustrated and feared his project request would be denied. We engaged in elements of the Kingdom Prayer Framework and ASKed how he could pitch this in a way that connected with the heart of his new manager. God gave him a really novel idea. Our client did it, and his request was approved.*

This example shows positioning used as an employee. When your intent is not to manipulate people or do them harm, it is amazing how many heavenly options are available. As an element of the Kingdom Ecosystem of Profits, positioning increases favor so sales increase.

Some of you are trying to position yourselves in places where the Lord did not say to position yourself. You are trying to stuff God into a funnel, a Facebook® group where you do not belong, or maybe a massive advertising campaign because you are comparing yourself to everyone around you. I get it because I did it. *"Everyone is doing [marketing flavor of the month] right now, so I should be doing it, too."* Well, if God told you to do it, then do it, but if God did not tell you to do it, then *why* are you trying to twist the thing God gave you and put it under a bushel somewhere hoping that it is going to produce the light? Take that thing from under the bushel and set it on a hill so that it can be a bright light and lead people to you. The favor of God will find you; your moths will find your flame.

WHAT CAME FIRST?

Before moving to the last element, I want to take this sidebar about people, product, and positioning. I do not know about you, but for the longest time I had a very hard time figuring out what in the world I had, by way of products, and where in the world I should position my products. Let's just be clear, there are a million ways to market your business. There are a million things you probably could do in your business. There are a million things you could manufacture. How do you know what is right for you? You don't need a million. You just need one backed by all of Heaven. This is what God gave me that helped me, and I'm hoping that it is going to help you, too. He gives one of these three things **first**: He gives you the people; "This is who you sell to." He gives you the product; "This is what you sell." Or He gives you the position; "This is the platform where the people are." When God ignites innovation on the earth through entrepreneurs and business leaders, He always gives one of those things first, but I do not hear too many people talking about which one comes first. Some say to start with people. Some go straight to the product first. Some lean toward the position. What did He give you first?

If God gave you people first, then you must seek a deeper understanding about who they are. Some great ASK prompts are: Why are they important to you God? What is hindering their success? Lord, give me Your heart for them. Once you dive deep into understanding the heart of the people you are to serve, then you can parlay that into a conversation with the Lord about what their assignment is and partner with the angelic assigned to your people group.

You need to know who you are, what you are doing, and where God is strategically deploying you so that you can advance in your industry for the glory of God. Where do your people congregate? Where are they easily accessed? What platforms do you need to use to reach them? What message do you need to communicate to get their attention? Once you are aware of their needs and wants, you can create products to effectively serve them. Asking questions can reframe exactly what it is your clients need and to give it to them.

If He gave you the product first, then seek deeper understanding into the purpose of the product because the purpose of a thing reflects function of the creation. If He gave you a product, then what is the purpose? What is the function? What did Heaven have in mind when He gave you this product idea? Because again, it was God's idea. What is the way, truth, and life of this product? What is the method around this product that is going to make it interesting? What is the truth that this product perpetuates, demonstrates, or underscores? Maybe there is a question on the flipside of that: what is the lie that this product disproves? What is the life in this product? Why is this important? What problem does this product solve? What need does this product meet? What "want" does this product satisfy?

As you are asking the Lord about the product that He is asking you to steward, consider the unique spin that your product has, and how it reflects the wonderful and positive parts of God. Who are the people who would benefit from this particular need being met in this particular way? Who are the people that capture your heart?

The Pray the Kingdom Way Course was an example of a product God gave to me first before He gave the people or the position. I began seeking by asking, "What is the purpose of this product? What is the purpose of this course? What is the way, truth, and life of this product? How do You want this product delivered? How do You want me to show up for this product? Who are the people attached to this? Who are the people who would love to hear this information? What is the best way to get in front of these people?"

I approached my team and told them we were not doing any more challenges, that we would be moving on to courses. I did this out of excitement and before I was finished seeking. I knew the people for my product were Kingdom business owners. When I began seeking the platform for positioning, the Lord told me to do a Profitable Prayer Challenge. Because I had previously spoken to them out of excitement, and not out of preparation, I had to humble myself, go back to my team, and redirect. This is not something I was fond of doing because redirection sometimes causes chaos and confusion, and my team is very important to me.

Once we were able to course correct, the blueprint for the Profitable Prayer Challenge came about. We were instructed through prayer to break down myths in the challenge in order to set the foundation for the course. We knew that what we were going to release with the course would come up against the lies that people had been believing, lies that would keep some from receiving the course well.

For me, the product came first, then the people, and finally the position. We began praying into advertising for the challenge for a way that would best utilize our gifts and talents. One of the solutions we obtained from Heaven was to go live with our closest friends and clients and talk about prayer for business. Through that we connected deeply with people we already knew and exposed them to our audience. I did fifteen one-hour interviews in one week and stood on the platforms of those nearest and dearest, and I got people from their audience to sign up for our challenge. We connected with Heaven for the unlimited resources and strategies that He had waiting for us.

If He gave you the position first, seek a deeper understanding of the platform posture or place that He is telling you to explore. Maybe some of you feel called to LinkedIn®, or maybe Instagram®, or YouTube®, or a podcast is more your thing. Maybe it is more about how you position your messaging in the marketplace Maybe a live event is in your heart, or a small group, or a conference or summit. That is the position, the place, the platform that He is telling you to explore. . Once God has given you the heart for position, inquire of Him about the people in that platform. What do they have in common? What do they want? What problems do they have? What needs must be met?

As you start hanging out there, you will see what the Holy Spirit is highlighting. Did you see that comment that person posted in the LinkedIn® group? Did you see that meme that somebody posted, or did you follow these people on Instagram®? There are plenty of social media groups for like-minded individuals, and maybe the Lord said to join a particular group. Once in the group, you may want to contribute, and you'll notice some themes. That is how you find your people. Holy Spirit, what are You highlighting? What do they have in common? What do they need? The product then stems from these interactions. How can You present something to them that will be helpful to their needs and wants?

For those of you who are struggling with one of these areas, I want you to ask yourself, what did God give you first? Go back to it. That is how you can be strategic in understanding where God is, because the enemy wants you to be confused; he wants you all over the place. He wants you to believe that you do not know your people or what they want. What did God give you first?

PROTECTION

Protection is one of the often overlooked aspects to profits. Any accountant or financial planner worth their salt will know many ways to protect money with insurance and guard against effects of inflation, taxes, etc. I encourage all businesspeople to have proper protection in place pertinent to their business and industry. Talk to the appropriate financial, insurance, and legal professionals so that money earned can turn into money that is kept and money that grows.

Another layer of protection that goes unnoticed is a spiritual one. God has safeguards and sentinels assigned to your business in the spirit realm. Power, principalities, and spiritual wickedness in high places exist and can influence us on Earth. Some of the struggles you face in your industry is because you are coming against the current power of the air. When a son or daughter of God shows up to shift the atmosphere and reclaim climates, the enemy doesn't go away quietly. Make no mistake, the enemy has to go because the greater one is in us, but it might try to flex on the way out. One of the reasons our clients come to us is because we acknowledge both the practical wisdom of business and the spiritual insights that affect business growth. The angelic is an unseen, yet very real, force that is operable in business. If you want to know more, I encourage you to find resources on understanding angels from a biblical perspective.

CASE STUDY: One of my clients came to us because his ethnic food restaurant had hit a money plateau and he wanted to know if there was anything going on in the spiritual realm. Using the Kingdom Prayer Framework, we sought God. The strategy that was revealed was a combination of prophetic acts to do in his restaurant and the releasing of the angelic assistance assigned to his business. We encouraged him to engage with God about releasing the angels to work on behalf of his restaurant. Within a matter of weeks, a local reporter who'd promised to do a story on the restaurant but had essentially ghosted them, reached back out, and printed the story. The following month, they had the highest revenue money in the history of their business. This was February 2020 and we all know what happened in March 2020—a pandemic hit the US that eviscerated businesses, especially restaurants. The unusually high revenue they made the previous month kept their restaurant from going under during the pandemic. It kept them afloat until other financial provisions became available. As of the time of this writing, his restaurant is back open and in full operation.

God supernaturally provided protection both spiritually and physically.

CASE STUDY: Another client who had made money online came to us when a major passive income stream from an ad account on a social media platform got shut down. They were perplexed because they didn't violate any of the rules. It was really hopeless, and they had no expectation that anything could be done. Using the elements of the Kingdom Prayer Framework, we ASKed and LISTENed. What is really going on? In the spirit we saw a vision of what looked like demonic dust bunnies, eating the ethernet cord of his computer. We pressed in and engaged in more TALK ♦ ASK ♦ LISTEN™ for further understanding. We heard insight into the demonic strategy of the enemy. And I ASKed God, "So what do you want to do about it?" We were instructed to craft a decree over his business that broke the connection in the spirit. It was a very powerful decree freeing technology from decay. After we did that, we ASKed God, "now what?" It was done in the spirit, but the ad account was still down, which meant the income was not coming in. The next phase was a practical one. We gave him some insights about who to ask for help. That person had some inside connection to the platform. He did it, and the ad account was restored.

We see the protection of God to protect the territory of their assignment. There is partnership between the spiritual realm and the physical realm. To this day, I still remember how funny it was to me how casual and nonchalant God's answer was. God was not phased. Jesus was straight chillin'. I was a little nervous. This seemed like an impossible situation, and I almost regretted taking on the task for the client. My faith in the circumstance was greater than the faith of God's provision. That is, until we heard from Heaven. We didn't just rebuke the devil in the name of Jesus and hope for the best. We got precise, surgical insight into this situation, and it was marvelous. I had been raised to think that fighting demons was hard and tiring work. It's not when you stand and operate with authority. This was insight from a place of authority that worked. It worked because of God, not because of the magic words.

CASE STUDY: Another client owned a marketing agency. In passing, she mentioned her excitement about a joint venture deal with another business. Things were going very well, and our client didn't talk to us about that deal. It wasn't the focus of our engagement at the time. One day, in prayer for this client, we got the sense that this other business was not being honest with our client. Our first inclination was to tell the client what we sensed, but Holy Spirit said DON'T. We were told not to say anything. I didn't like this directive at all. But our direction was clear not to say anything. We ASKed if we were to release anything by way of decree and declaration. NOPE. It felt like we were benched with very important information. We had to trust God. Then our client came to us and said, "I have a bad feeling about [insert business name] and our deal." She shared a dream she had and the sense that she got from it. She was perplexed because she remembered getting the green light from God to pursue this. So why the warning now? It was then that we were released to share the insight we got, and she ended the deal with no issues.

I will never forget the lessons from that client interaction. God was protecting her and increasing her discernment, and had we disobeyed and shared out of timing, it would have interrupted her growth. As great as we are at what we do for our clients—helping them unlock practical and spiritual tactics for wealth in business—Brave will never take the place of God, Jesus, or Holy Spirit. We will never willingly allow a client to rely on us more than they rely on God, Jesus, or Holy Spirit. In fact, we had to release some clients because they began to form unhealthy attachments to us. We refused some clients because they wanted us to use our prophetic insight as a magical way to get over on people or bypass legal ways to obtain riches. Not on my watch.

Each case study I shared in this book used parts of the Kingdom Prayer Framework differently, but they all achieved a level of success God intended. For most, it was financial because businesses are supposed to make money, and others were personal because God loves people. As a framework, it is broad to allow for specifics.

When people ask me about specific prayer modalities, going into the courts of Heaven, or spiritual warfare practices, I don't answer the way they want. If you want me to tell you to do or not do one modality over another, I won't. I present the framework from which those modalities originated. I see them as tools that God can use to inform us of our position and authority to deepen our understanding. I will never exalt the practices of a modality over relationship with Jesus. Jesus did many miracles, and often they had the same outcome without using the same method. He healed blind eyes with words, dirt, and spit. He healed with garments and river washing. We tend to look at the methods and focus on reproducing those without understanding that they only worked because of their relationship to Jesus.

CONVENTIONAL WISDOM

A note about conventional wisdom. First of all, let's stop acting like conventional wisdom and the wisdom of man did not come from God.

When people talk about conventional wisdom or the wisdom of man, they are really talking about a rhema revelation someone got a long time ago that with refinement became operational in the earth with such consistency that it is now the norm. This is how the Kingdom is supposed to work. If the Lord tells you to use conventional wisdom, then use conventional wisdom because there is grace on it, and He said to use it. But *if* He has given you something else, do not buck, block, or tune Him out because you esteem a conventional wisdom higher than the One who created wisdom.

UNAPOLOGETIC

How do you unapologetically pray for profits? You just do it. Unapologetic means without regret or remorse. The question is what is preventing you from being unapologetic? Could it be something you incorrectly believe about God, or yourself, the situation? Identify what it is and TALK to God about it. I used to be apologetic for so many things. The remorse that I felt was directly tied to "worthiness." I apologized for things that didn't need apologizing. To this day, I still catch myself saying "sorry" when what I really meant was, "excuse me" or "could you repeat that" or " I don't understand." I apologized so people would like me and think I was humble. I apologized because I knew but for the grace of God, there go I. My husband and I were virgins when we married not because we hadn't tried to lose our virginity. The opportunities presented themselves, trust me. And yet, I still felt apologetic. I stayed in positions and places longer than I needed to because I was "sorry" about the deficit I would put the leader in if I left. I apologized, for raising my prices. I remember I was on a sales call and I quoted the person a price that was too low. I was in the process of raising my prices and when the time came to present the new price, I flaked and quoted her the lower price. She agreed to the lower price. I didn't feel great that I closed the sale. I felt horrible. In some quick TALK ♦ ASK ♦ LISTEN™, I realized I needed to call the lady back and give her my new price. I was so nervous. *What would she think of me?* But in my TALK, Wisdom told me how to frame the conversation. And more importantly, what I was supposed to learn from this incident. I called her back. She picked up right away. I said something to the effect of, *"I had to call you back because I made an error. I quoted you the incorrect price for the service. The correct price is blah blah. However, because of my error, I will still perform the service at the price I originally quoted. I just wanted to be honest with you about what happened."* Know what happened next? She agreed to pay the higher price. Then she remarked how the act of me calling her back and taking a stand on my price taught her a lesson as a business owner as well. I am very empathetic in nature, but I had to learn to submit my empathy to the Lordship of Christ. That doesn't mean I became stone cold, but it meant that I had to learn to discern when my empathy and compassion for others was getting in the way of what God was doing in people's lives. In 1 Kings 17, Elijah told the widow woman to make Him a meal first. This was after she'd just told him that she was gathering sticks to make one last meal for her and her son before they die. How compassionless of the prophet, right? No, the prophet had a word from the Lord that was greater than her present pain. If the widow heeded the instruction, she would be blessed for many days. In business, we've all heard the "I can't afford it" objection. The temptation for kind hearted people is to discount the price. For some of you this is not the issue. Maybe your issue with being unapologetic has to do with working with a brand, celebrity, company or person that is not well liked or regarded. Some of you are shifting from being in one industry or having a program or service that is still in demand to closing it down to follow the leading of the Lord. This is why TALK ♦ ASK ♦ LISTEN™ is so important in business. Before you make moves, make sure you are doing it in alignment with what Heaven says. Some of you are being trained up in a way that will require you to deal with the next generation, but if your mouth is always fighting the new, how can you ever do that? Being unapologetic is not the same as getting on a soapbox to vent. Being unapologetic is not the same as being demanding. During the pandemic, so many people made the restrictions and the vaccine about personal choice, having their rights infringed on by the government, or the mistrust of science. I don't care what your stance was or is on that. But how many people, regardless of their personal convictions, prayed about what God was doing on the earth irrespective of the pandemic or the vaccine? We can complain about the news and its biases, but how many are engaged in TALK ◆ ASK ◆ LISTEN™ for what the Lord is wanting to do and how He he wants to do it? Right now, artificial intelligence is the trend with services like Jasper and ChatGPT being touted as both the next best thing and the beginning of the end, depending who you talk to. I am not interested in arguments. I'm interested in what God is doing in His business leaders, inventors, innovators, trailblazers and pioneers on the earth and my role in helping them step fully into destiny. I hold no remorse for that assignment.

In order to be unapologetic, perspective shifts might require conversations with the Lord, deliverance, education, and therapy. I had to get counseling and therapy for some deep seated issues. And let me tell you, the tone and contents of my TALK when I was in therapy would straight offend some church folk, but it never offended God. That is when I learned that my breakthrough is on the other side of my honesty.

When you understand how to *Pray the Kingdom Way*, you become unapologetic and bold in praying for any and everything, including goo-gobs of money. I don't feel ashamed or guilty about praying for profits because I know I am praying for the ecosystem of profits to sustain and thrive. I am not motivated by money or proving haters wrong. I have come, like Jesus, to do what I see my Father doing and to say what my Father is saying, no matter what He says about me, money, or business. My job isn't to hold the world ransom to the lies we've seen in operation but to set it free. I understand the Kingdom's purpose of business, so I am unapologetic about being in business. I understand the Kingdom's purpose for money, so I am unapologetic about inviting money into my collection and disbursement centers, aka bank accounts. I am unapologetic about praying for people, products, positioning, sales, etc., so I expect righteousness in these areas. I am no longer convinced that I am an evil villain capable of messing up the will of God. No, I am a daughter, heir, co-creator, and powerful force. It is time to stop apologizing for being called to be great, to make a lot of money, and to impact the world. One of my coaches, Darnyelle Jervey Harmon, often says, "You can make a dollar and a difference." You cannot unapologetically pray for profits if you are secretly sorry or scared. You are called by God to exist on this level; embrace it in your heart. Otherwise, it won't work without you. Be unapologetic. The best strategies come from the right relationships, so what is your relationship to God? With yourself? Your business? Your money? Which people has He released to you? What is He saying to you about them and what they need? The answers are available to these and all questions. All you have to do is pray the Kingdom way.

Pray the Kingdom Way Prayer Prompt #7: *Ask Holy Spirit, "What is something that I am apologizing for that I shouldn't be apologizing for? What is one thing I can do today to become more unapologetic?"*

AFTERWORD

BUSINESS LEADERS RISE UP!

In the beginning of this book, I shared how a question *from* God can change your life. By now, I hope you see how a question *to* God has the potential to do the same. When asked if He could teach me to pray, I was seasoned in prayer, yet there was an upgrade available. For those seasoned in prayer, this book showed you how to be more precise and accurate in praying for "bigger" and more complex issues. For those newer in prayer, this book gave you a super simple way to pray more often without worrying if you are doing it right.

As you read this book, you probably noticed that you already use some parts of the framework. This means you can focus on the other parts. In teaching this content for the past few years, I found that people TALK ◆ ASK ◆ LISTEN™ more than they realize. What is missing are the DECREEs co-created from the heart of God, not our opinions of what's needed. With knowledge of the *Pray The Kingdom Way* framework, I hope you are excited and encouraged to bring your *Judea, Jerusalem, and Samria* to God to see how He is using you to point the way to wholeness as a guardian to your sphere of influence. How much more effective could we be if we sought His will on Earth as it is in Heaven from fully healed and healthy perspectives on all things? This framework shows how exciting it is co-creating with God anytime, anywhere for anything. I hope this book serves to strengthen your confidence as you grow. For those in business, hopefully this book served as a conversation starter with God about your view of your business and money.

Praying without ceasing is no longer a lifelong accusation of how much you and I miss the mark when we *Pray The Kingdom Way*. This book is a great foundation for crafting decrees that you can profess over yourself, your business, your family, your city etc. You will want to pray more when you realize that your good and loving Father always answers prayer.

Business Owner Arise

> *Be strong and courageous, for you are the one who will lead these people to possess all the land I swore to their ancestors I would give them.* **(Joshua 1:6 NLT)**

In closing, I want to specifically talk to the owners, entrepreneurs, and pioneers. It is time to rise up and take your seat of authority in your sphere of influence.

There is a fable about a farmer who, while out walking, found an egg. He picked up the egg and brought it back to his farm and placed it in his chicken's nest with the other chicken eggs. The egg hatched alongside the other chicken eggs. The egg the farmer had found was different from all the other chickens. Nonetheless, the newly hatched bird looked around, and did what it saw the other birds doing. One day an eagle was flying overhead and let out a screech. The bird looked up because there was something about the sound of the eagle's screech that resonated deep inside it. It looked around but the other chickens did not respond to the sound. It heard it again. It turns out the egg the farmer found was an eagle's egg. And though it had been raised as a chicken to peck, scratch, and fly low like a chicken, the moment it heard the sound of what it was meant to be, something changed everything in it. It had been awakened to its dormant identity and thus its ability to soar high above the cloud, navigate jet streams, and command the sky.

Pray The Kingdom Way is my clarion call to Kingdom business owners/leaders. It is designed to awaken you to your dormant identities and compel you to possess new land. If you have read this far, it means there was something inside you that resonated and, dare I say, longed for what you just read. Though it challenged your thinking, there were so many things that made sense.

The scriptures say, *"they that have an ear, let them hear."* Like that eaglet, you have a choice to make. You can chalk this book up as just another one you read that stirred you, but you do nothing with the stirring. You can go back to your life as a business owner desiring to advance the Kingdom of God through business but telling yourself, "It's someone else's job" or "Who am I to do this?" You can go back to being among others who, although the call was made, did not respond to it. You can go back to trying to do business the world's way with a little Jesus sauce on top. But you already know how that is going to end. You will still be seeking a year from now.

OR...

You can lean into everything that stirred you in reading this book and look at it as a foundation for the change that you are experiencing—you as His child, you as a business owner, you as a leader who is sensing the move God is doing in the business world. And the truth of the matter is, like Joshua 1:6, you have a part to play in leading people to possess the land God already ordained for them to have. It begins with accepting the fact that you are called to do it.

How can I make such a claim? Because you would not have read this far in this book if God was not preparing you to have a great impact in the business world. *Pray The Kingdom Way* is the foundational understanding for business owners to unapologetically possess their possessions without being obsessed with possessions.

With the Kingdom Prayer Framework as a foundation, let me present what's next. The whole point is to awaken you so that you arise to your identity, align to your assignment, attain your territory, and ascend to legacy. These are the pillars of a business's Spiritual Operations System™. That is the framework we use at Brave Leadership Consulting to help Kingdom business owners turn their awareness of what God is doing into actionable steps that produce results. *Pray the Kingdom Way* is the instrument through which you learn how to govern on Earth as it is in Heaven. God is doing a move in business, especially among prophetic leaning Kingdom entrepreneurs, to help them advance in areas of business to be more visible, make more money, and have more impact. Why? Because the goal is legacy. The scripture says that God created everything to reproduce after its own kind. So, God is raising up a hoard of businesswomen and men to be mothers and fathers of industries and sectors to teach others how to be mother and father industries and sectors.

I refer back to the vision of a skyscraper in a business district with the phone receiver on top. God has positioned His face to the receiver to talk to businesses. Will you position yourself to recognize the connection that already exists and listen?

But once you recognize, will you amplify? Because the next step is to occupy and advance. If you are like me, you are tired of talking about possessions and promises. You want to see them possessed. But as Kingdom business owners, God is *not* allowing us to advance and occupy based on hustle, grind, and presumption. We must understand His reason and purpose for possessing so we are not caught up in ego, pride, and self-aggrandizement. If we are called to be reformers, which we are, then our methods of reformation must be heavenly ones.

Pray The Kingdom Way is the foundation that undergirds every Spiritual Operations System™ God wants to install in every business to see the ROI on Earth as it is in Heaven. Will you take your place and lead people to possess? Let's do it together.

If you are a business leader, Founder/CEO, or just pioneering something new, and you want to partner with the prophetic, activate your business's spiritual authority, and welcome more wealth, you need to contact me.

If you are a business owner looking to partner with the prophetic, activate your authority and welcome more wealth, reach out to me. I have given example after example of how parts of the framework were used to help businesses get breakthroughs. Are you next? If you want to work with me, have me come speak on your podcast, show, at your in person or virtual event, reach out. Visit www.BraveLeadershipConsulting.com or direct inquiries to info@braveleadershipconsulting.com. I look forward to co-creating with you as you co-create with God!

APPENDIX

Figure 1: Kingdom Prayer Framework

Kingdom Prayer Framework

TALK ♦ ASK ♦ LISTEN ♦ DECLARE ♦ DECREE

CONNECTION
in Heaven

for

CO-CREATION
on Earth

© 2023 Brave Leadership Consulting
www.BraveLeadershipConsulting.com

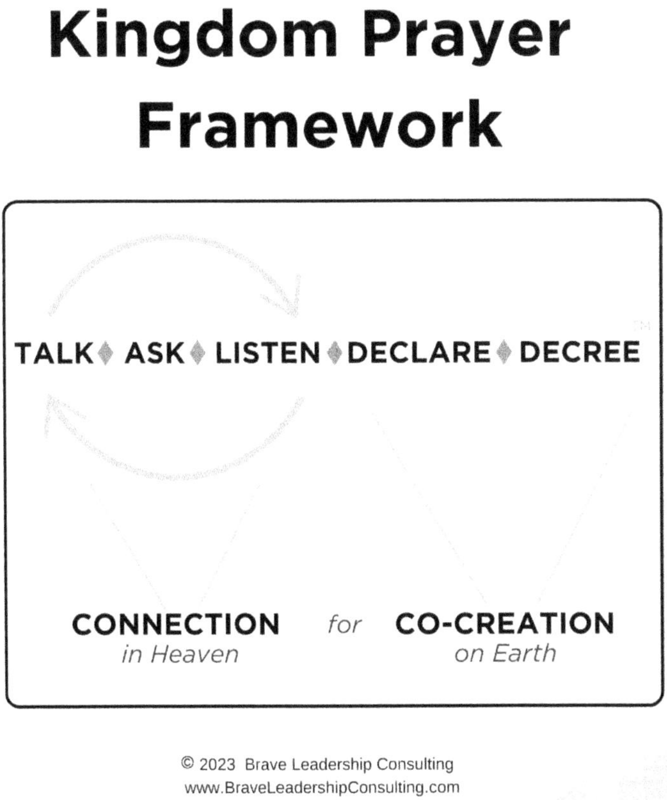

Figure 2: Heavenly Influence on Earth

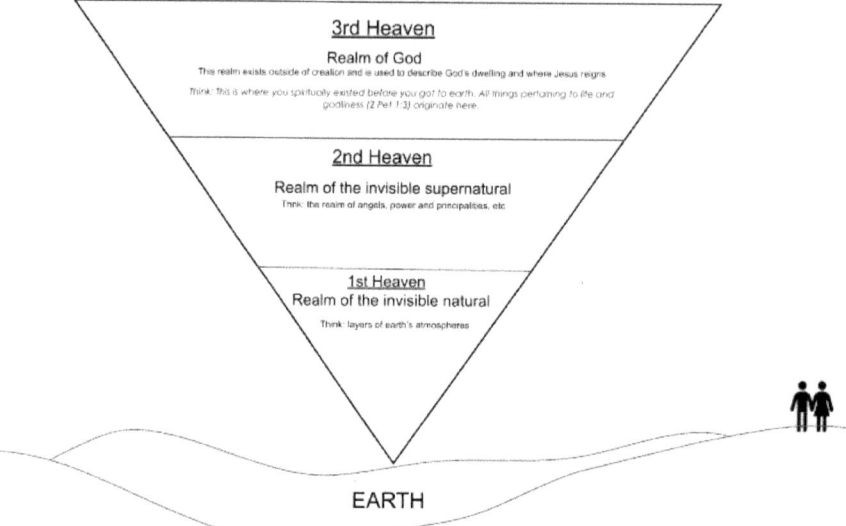

Prayer Workbook Sample Page | 161

TOPIC List one topic	I want to talk to you about... or A decision needs to be made about...
TALK Empty Yourself Out	Write down ALL your thoughts, feelings, beliefs, concerns etc. about the TOPIC.
ASK Receive His Thoughts	ASK His perspective on TOPIC: Use Your Favorite Ask Prompt To Ignite Your Listening (See Appendix)
LISTEN Capture What He Says	LISTEN for what He says: Write down what you hear, see, or feel.

©2023 Brave Leadership Consulting, LLC | Do Not Reproduce Without Written Permission from Brave Leadership Consulting

TOPIC List one topic	I want to talk to you about... or A decision needs to be made about...
TALK Empty Yourself Out	Write down ALL your thoughts, feelings, beliefs, concerns etc. about the TOPIC.
ASK Receive His Thoughts	ASK His perspective on TOPIC: Use Your Favorite Ask Prompt To Ignite Your Listening (See Appendix)
LISTEN Capture What He Says	LISTEN for what He says: Write down what you hear, see, or feel.

©2023 Brave Leadership Consulting, LLC | Do Not Reproduce Without Written Permission from Brave Leadership Consulting

TALK Some More	Write down ALL your thoughts about what He just said
ASK Some More	ASK Repeat question or Ask NEW question(s) based on what He just said. (See Appendix)
LISTEN Some More	LISTEN for further insight or clarification: Write down what you hear, see, or feel.

©2023 Brave Leadership Consulting, LLC | Do Not Reproduce Without Written Permission from Brave Leadership Consulting

DECLARE Let It Be Known	DECLARE what He says about Himself or about you. (What scripture, name or characteristic of Father, Son, or Holy Spirit needs to rule over this topic or be made known? What truth about you needs to be made known?)
DECREE Legislate From Heaven	DECREE it into the earth. (Based on our conversation, what do you want me to decree regarding this topic to see movement on earth)

©2023 Brave Leadership Consulting, LLC | Do Not Reproduce Without Written Permission from Brave Leadership Consulting

Additional Note Space

125+ PRAY THE KINGDOM WAY ASK PROMPTS

These prompts can be applied to anything you want to TALK to God about. They're categorized, but multiple prompts can fit multiple categories. These are all designed to jump start conversation between you and God. Place a check ✓ mark beside the ones you use. Highlight the ones that prompted the most insightful conversation.

Connection Prompts

(When you have no agenda of your own and just want to know what's on His mind)

- I want to talk about your goodness, where shall I begin?
- What do you want to talk to me about today?
- What is on your heart?
- What is something you've been wanting to talk about, but I've been putting it off?
- How would you like me to see you?
- What territory are you expanding into now?
- How can I come into agreement with what you are currently doing?
- What are you pleased with?
- What is grieving you?
- What do you want to see more of?
- What do you want to see less of?
- What do you think about this?
- What are you doing?
- What do you want to do?
- What is important to you?

- What makes you smile?
- Jesus, what are you interceding for?
- Holy spirit, what are you teaching?
- What scripture do I meditate on?

Growth/ Renewing Your Mind/ Increase Understanding Prompts
(When you want to grow or need to accept a new way of thinking)

- How did you equip me to handle this?
- What do I need to change my mind about, so I see this differently?
- What do I need to release or let go of in order to see this situation differently?
- What is distracting me from growing deeper in you?
- What am I ignoring because I think it's too painful/hard, but you've given grace for it?
- What do you think about this?
- What perspective do I need to have to see success?
- What is going on behind the scenes?
- If I wasn't hurt/offended/ afraid, how would I approach this?
- What is your promise in this?
- What does the scripture say about this?
- What scripture have I misunderstood or misapplied?
- What would be the wisest thing?
- Why do I keep procrastinating on this?
- What is preventing me from being consistent?
- Where am I relying too much on my effort and not enough on yours?
- Where am I relying too much on your effort and not enough on mine?
- I don't have a good feeling about this, tell me why?
- I don't like or trust this person, what should I do about this?
- Is it me?

Unstuck Prompts
(When you feel stagnant, or something isn't moving)

- What's something you told me to do that I forgot you told me to do?
- What perspective do I need to have to see success?

- What does unstuck look like right now?
- Am I really stuck?
- What is the solution?
- What do I need to ask?
- What do I need to know?
- Who has the solution?
- What does wisdom say?
- How is this already finished and handled in heaven?
- What is the timing for this?
- What do I need to ignore?
- What haven't I paid enough attention to?
- What do I need to repent of?
- How have I pushed past the grace you've given me for this?
- What boundary did you set up for protection?
- What am I afraid of?
- Do I stand and resist or yield?
- Who do I need to forgive?
- What do I need to forgive?
- What have I assumed to be true, but is not?
- What lie is keeping me from moving forward?
- What am I afraid to give or surrender to you?

Declare/ Worship Prompts
(When you want to profess who He is or when you need to profess who you are)

- What are you teaching me about you in this?
- What's one of your names that you want me to focus on?
- What attribute can I worship today?
- What do you want me to declare about myself?
- How have you been better to me than I realize?
- What perspective of you do I need to keep front and center?

Decree/Co-Creation Prompts
(When you are ready to make commands from Heaven that change earth)

- What do I release?
- What do you want me to say to make this shift?
- What do I say to reinforce what you are already doing?
- What needs to be repeated on Earth as it is in Heaven?

- What does the finished work of the cross demand I say about this?
- What do I say that would release righteousness?
- What do I say that would release peace?
- What do I say that would release joy?
- What do I say that would set things in proper order?
- What atmospheric shift needs to happen?
- What do I release to make way for what you want to accomplish?
- What do I say to create what you want to create?

Expansion/ Offensive Prompts
(When you want to proactively take territory or expand)

- Who else needs to be involved in this?
- What opportunity or activity is ready for me now?
- What do I need to prepare now for?
- How does this demonstrate your love?
- How does this show your goodness?
- What does the next level of this look like?
- What deal do I need to make that I am not making?
- What connection or partnership do I need to have for this?
- What connection or partnership do I need to lose so I can keep growing?
- What is your wildest dream for this?
- What do I do today that will make 30 days from now look better?
- What do I do today that will make 60 days from now look better?
- What do I do today that will make 90 days from now look better?
- What do I do today that will make 180 days from now look better?
- What do I do today that will make a year from now look better?
- What new territory have you opened to me?

- What is the timing for what you are doing?
- What is a product I can create that will make me lots of money?
- Is there a credential that I need for where I am going?
- What do I need to be persistent in pursuing?
- How can I think bigger?

Defensive Prompts
(When you want to defend or protect)

- What is preventing this?
- What is holding this back?
- What is blocking this?
- What is allowing fear to show up and stay?
- What is a problem that is coming that I need to prepare for?
- What problems do I tend to fall for and why?
- What stigma, prejudice, or incorrect thinking am I coming up against?
- What do I need to protect and how do I protect it?

Profit prompts
(When you want to get insight into business situations)

- What is your intent for this?
- How do I communicate this the most effectively?
- What is the price of this?
- What is the right price point for the greatest overall profit?
- What is the amount you want me to ask for, but I am too nervous to ask for?
- Where can I find the people you've equipped to be on my team?
- What platform best serves this message?
- What platform do I need to be on?
- What platform can I ignore right now?
- What is the money goal?
- Where is the money?
- Who has the capacity for this?
- What do I need to let go?
- What does success look like?
- What vehicles do I put my money in?

- What can I take away that would make me more profitable?
- How can I treat my people better?
- How can I improve our product's reliability?
- What would make our customers happier?
- What can we do to gain more business?
- What do we need to stop doing to gain more business?
- What resources would increase my ability to lead?
- What equipment do I need to acquire to make us more efficient?
- What tools do I need to grow?
- Is there anything I need that I'm ignoring just because it is not my preference?
- How can I give more?
- How can I improve my relationship with money?
- What skills or talents am I underutilizing in my people?
- What opportunity is my team ready for that I'm not seeing?
- Where is the money leaking?
- Why is the money leaking?
- What am I spending my money on that I don't need to spend money on?
- If money flows, what can I do to have more of it flow our way?
- What is the profit goal?
- Is it time to take a break?
- What spiritual resources do I need to tap into?
- What angelic power is already assigned to make this great?
- Who do I need to trust more?
- Who do I need to rely on less?
- How can I have more fun?
- What is the rhythm of rest I need to maintain?

Your Own Prompts

-
-
-

ABOUT THE AUTHOR

Julia M. Winston is a prophetic Executive Advisor, Coach, and Consultant to Kingdom advancing Founders, CEOs, entrepreneurs, and leaders in business.

Unlike others who are focused on teaching you their way of success, Julia is dedicated to helping you chart your success course based on who God says you are, what you carry, and where you are to unleash it.

Julia has done leadership development and coaching work for individuals and organizations such as GE, Chick-Fil-A, The US Department of Agriculture, City Municipalities, Fisk University, The University of Mississippi, and Baptist Hospital.

Julia is a former member of the Forbes Coaches Council. She holds two coaching certifications. She also has a Master's Degree in Human Resource Development. She is an award-winning keynote speaker and trainer.

Julia M. Winston is wisdom powerfully personified and strategically unleashed for success.

Julia draws on her decades of experience in leadership development, her spiritual journey of training business people in Kingdom understanding and prophetic expression, her love of movies and 90s music, and being behind the scenes helping top Kingdom influencers make millions. ***Julia is unmatched in her ability to help you identify, honor, and own the great assignment God has for you to do in the world.***

She is the CEO of Brave Leadership Consulting, the founder of The Alignment Advantage, the founder of The Insight Network, and the author of *Pray The Kingdom Way*. Through her advisory firm, she equips founder, CEOs, and business leaders to align their business to God's intent to see natural and supernatural success and satisfaction.

For more information about her advisory and consulting services, please email info@braveleadershipconsulting.com or visit www.BraveLeadershipConsulting.com.

www.ingramcontent.com/pod-product-compliance
Ingram Content Group UK Ltd.
Pitfield, Milton Keynes, MK11 3LW, UK
UKHW021312180426
11947UKWH00015B/1173